Warman's

Hummel®

FIELD GUIDE

Carl F. Luckey & Dean A. Genth

Values and Identification

©2004 Krause Publications

Published by

krause publications

An imprint of F+W Publications, Inc.

700 East State Street • Iola, WI 54990-0001
715-445-2214 • 888-457-2873
www.krause.com

Our toll-free number to place an order or obtain
a free catalog is (800) 258-0929.

The illustrations of M.I. Hummel art are printed in this collectors' guide under license by ARS AG, Baar/Switzerland. Neither ARS AG nor W. Goebel Porzellanfabrik are responsible for any information contained in this guide, in particular with regard to all quotations of prices.

M.I. Hummel®, and M.I. Hummel Club®, in signature and/or block forms, are registered trademarks of W. Goebel Porzellanfabrik GmbH & Co. KG, Germany.

M.I. Hummel figurines, plates, bells and other collectibles are copyrighted products. ©Goebel.

Library of Congress Catalog Number: 2004101560

ISBN: 0-87349-778-3

Designed by Stacy Bloch
Edited by Tracy L. Schmidt
Printed in the United States

Table of Contents

Photo Credits

The images on the following pages appear courtesy of Goebel of North America:

8, 16, 83, 85, 90, 132, 157, 169, 188, 189, 193, 197, 200, 202, 205, 208, 211, 215, 217, 219, 223, 226, 229, 232, 235, 238, 242-244, 246, 247, 249, 251-253, 255-257, 259, 261, 263-265, 267-269, 271-273, 275-277, 279, 280, 281, 283, 285, 287-289, 291-293, 295-297, 299, 300, 301, 303, 304, 307, 308, 309, 311-313, 315-317, 319-321, 323-327, 329, 331-333, 335-337, 339, 341-343, 345-349, 351-353, 355-357, 359, 360, 361, 363, 365-369, 371-373, 375-377, 379-381, 383-387, 389, 391, 393-397, 399-401, 403-405, 407-409, 411-413, 415-417, 419, 420, 421, 423-425, 427-429, 431-433, 435-437, 439-441, 443-445, 447-449, 451-453, 455-457, 459-461, 463-465, 467-469, 471-473, 475-477, 479-481, 483-485, 487-489, 491-493, 495, 497.

The images on the following pages appear courtesy of the M.I. Hummel Club: 22, 97, 99, 104 (top image).

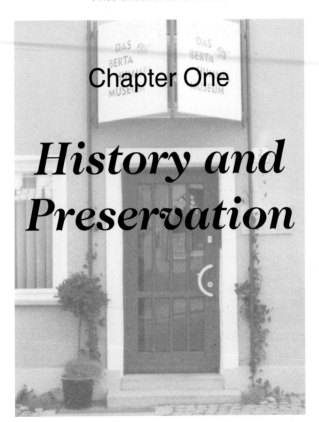

Chapter One

History and Preservation

Historical Overview

Sister Maria Innocentia (Berta) Hummel, 1909-1946

Sister of the Third Order of Saint Francis Siessen Convent, Saulgau, Germany

The story of the Hummel figurines is unique. It is practically required reading for those with an interest in the artist, her work, and the resulting three-dimensional fine earthenware renditions—the famous Hummel figurines.

These charming but simple figurines of boys and girls easily capture hearts. In them we see, perhaps, our son or daughter, sister or brother, or even ourselves when we were racing along the paths of happy childhood. When you see the School Boy or School Girl you may be taken back to your own school days. Seeing the figurine Culprits could bring back the time when you purloined your first apple from a neighbor's tree and were promptly chased away by his dog. You will delight in the beauty of the Flower Madonna or Shepherd's Boy. You will love them all with their little round faces and big questioning eyes. These figurines will collect you, and if you have the collecting tendency, you will undoubtedly want to collect them.

PROOF

A. Hummel

Berta Hummel, who later became known as Sister Maria Innocentia, as portrayed in a self-portait.

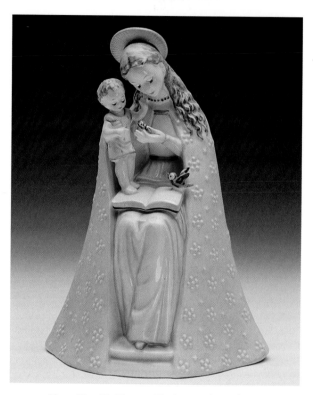

Hum No. 10 *Flower Madonna*, $230-$950

You may ask yourself what artist is behind these beguiling figurines. Who is the person with the talent to portray beauty and innocence with such simplicity? The answer is Berta Hummel, a Franciscan sister called Maria Innocentia.

Berta Hummel was born on May 21, 1909, in Massing in lower Bavaria, which was located about 40 miles northeast of Munich, Germany. She grew up in a family of two brothers and three sisters in a home where music and art were part of everyday life. In this environment, her talent for art was encouraged and nourished by her parents.

Hummel attended primary school between 1915 and 1921. During these early years, she demonstrated the great imagination so necessary for an artist. She created delightful little cards and printed verses for family celebrations, birthdays, anniversaries, and Christmas. Her subjects were almost always the simple objects with which she was familiar: flowers, birds, animals, and her friends. In her simple child's world, she saw only the beautiful things around her.

When she finished primary school, Hummel was enrolled in the Girls Finishing School in Simbach in 1921, in order to nurture and train her talent further and to give her a wider scope of education and experience. Here again, her artistic talent was recognized and upon finishing, it was decided

M.J.Hummel®

Facsimilie of the well-known M.I. Hummel signature.

that she should go to a place where she could further cultivate that talent and realize her desire to pursue art as a vocation. In 1927, Hummel moved to Munich, where she entered the Academy of Fine and Applied Arts. There she lived the life of an artist, made friends, and painted to her heart's content. At the academy, she acquired full mastery of art history, theory, and technique. It was here also that she met two Franciscan sisters who, like herself, attended the academy.

There is an old adage that art and religion go together. Berta Hummel's life was no exception. She became friends with the two sisters and began to think that this might be the best way to serve. Over time, she decided to join the sisters in their pilgrimage for art and God, in spite of the fact that she had been offered a position at the academy.

For a time, Hummel divided her days between her talent for art and her love for humanity and hours of devotion and worship. Then she took the first step into a new life of sacrifice and love. After completing her term as a novice, the 25-year-old took the first vows in the Convent of Siessen on August 30, 1934.

Although Berta Hummel (now Sister Maria Innocentia) gave her life over to an idea she thought greater than any worldly aspiration, the world became the recipient of her wonderful works. Within the walls and the beautiful surroundings of the centuries-old convent, she created the paintings and drawings that were to make her famous. Within these sacred confines, her artistic desires enjoyed unbounded impetus.

Little did her superiors dream that this modest blue-eyed artist who had joined their community would someday win worldwide renown. Much less did they realize what financial assistance Hummel's beloved convent would derive from her work as an artist.

During World War II, in 1945, after the French had occupied the region, the noble-minded artist's state of health was broken. On November 6, 1946, at age 37, despite the best care, God summoned her to His eternal home, leaving all her fellow sisters in deep mourning.

Today, the M.I. Hummel figurines, modeled according to Sister Maria Innocentia's work, are known all over the world. They are her messengers, bringing pleasure to many, many people.

Merry Wanderer (Hum 7), one of the original 46
figurines released by Goebel in 1935, and one
of the most collectible figurines today, $330-$25,000.

W. Goebel Porzellanfabrik

In an area very near Coburg in northern Bavaria, Franz Detleff Goebel and his son William Goebel founded the company in 1871. Once known as Oeslau, the village is now known as Rodental.

Initially, the company manufactured slates, pencils, and marbles, and after 1879, it was well into the production of porcelain dinnerware and beer steins.

By the mid-1910s, a third generation, Max Louis Goebel, had taken the helm of the company and it began manufacturing fine earthenware products. His son, Franz Goebel, became active in the company, and the two of them developed a line of porcelain figurines that was well accepted on the international market.

Upon Max Louis' death in 1929, Franz took over the running of the company along with his brother-in-law Dr. Eugen Stocke, a trained economist, who was the financial manager of the operation.

By the early 1930s, Goebel had gained considerable experience and expertise in fashioning products of porcelain and fine earthenware.

Sister Maria Innocentia's art came to the attention of Franz in December 1933 in the form of religious note cards for the Christmas and New Year seasons. These cards were brand-new publications of her art by Ars Sacra Josef Muller Verlag. (This company has since evolved into Ars AG, well known to collectors of prints and postcards of Hummel art.)

Remarkably, it was in March of the same year that the Siessen Convent had made an unsolicited inquiry of the Josef Muller firm regarding the possibility of reproducing their Sister Maria Innocentia's art.

Once Franz Goebel saw the cards in Munich, he conceived the idea of translating them into three-dimensional figurines. He sought and gained permission from the convent and Sister Maria Innocentia Hummel. The original letters rest in the Goebel archives. The letter granting Goebel permission stated plainly that all proposed designs must be preapproved before the product could be manufactured. This is true to this day: The convent still has the final say as to whether a proposed design stays within the high standards insisted upon by M.I. Hummel.

After Franz Goebel gained permission for the company to produce the figurines, it took about a year to model the first examples, make the first molds, experiment with media, and make the first models of fine earthenware. The company presented the first figurines at the Leipzig Fair in 1935. They were a great success, and by the end of 1935, there were 46 models in the new line of Hummel figurines.

Production of Hummel figurines—and practically everything else in the Goebel lines—slowly dwindled during the years of World War II, and toward the end of the war, production had ceased completely. During the American Occupation, the United States Military Occupation Government allowed Goebel to resume operation. This, of course, included the production of Hummel figurines. During this period, the figurines became quite popular among U.S. servicemen in the occupation forces, and upon their return to the states, many brought them home as gifts. This activity engendered a new popularity for Hummel figurines.

Today, W. Goebel Porzellanfabrik maintains a large factory complex in Rodental, where it manufactures, among many other things, M.I. Hummel figurines and related articles. The company maintains a very nice visitor center where it welcomes collectors. Visitors are shown a film and then taken on a short tour to view the manufacturing process in a special demonstration room.

Museums and Institutions

The Donald E. Stephens Museum of Hummels

The Donald E. Stephens Museum of Hummels was opened in 1986 in the Rosemont Exposition Center. Stephens, longtime mayor of Rosemont, Illinois, donated his magnificent Hummel collection to the village in 1984 for the purpose of establishing a museum.

Exterior view of the Donald E. Stephens Museum of Hummels in Rosemont, Illinois.

The 15,000-square-foot museum, located just five minutes from Chicago's O'Hare International Airport, is probably the largest public display in the world of both the current-production M.I. Hummel items and the old, rare pieces. The collection does not stop there, however. It is constantly expanding. With guidance from the board of directors and with Stephens' expert consulting, the museum continues to seek out and acquire rare pieces.

Interior view of the Donald E. Stephens Museum of Hummels.

The museum is large enough to accommodate the Stephens Collection, a display of all current M.I. Hummel products, a facsimile Goebel factory that demonstrates the fashioning of the figurines, a display of other Goebel products, a display of ANRI figurines, special exhibits and shows, a retail store (known as The Village Gift Shop), and an auditorium.

The Donald E. Stephens Museum of Hummels is open to the public with free admission and parking. The address is: Donald E. Stephens Convention Center—Lobby, 5555 North River Road, Rosemont, Illinois 60018. It is advisable to call for hours and/or to arrange a group visit: (847) 692-4000. The museum's Web site is: www. stephenshummelmuseum.com.

Das Berta-Hummel-Museum im Hummelhaus

This museum was opened in July 1994. It is located in the Hummel home in Massing, Bavaria, and was the birthplace of Berta Hummel and her home, before she took her vows to become a nun.

The museum, directed by her nephew Alfred Hummel, houses the largest exhibit of Hummel figurines in Europe. More important is the large

**A view of the entry to the Berta-Hummel-Museum
in Massing, Germany.**

collection of paintings and drawings the artist
accomplished before entering the convent. The
museum and a related pre-existing company have
been responsible for the production of several

**An interior view showing some of
Berta Hummel's artwork.**

**An interior view showing some of
Berta Hummel's artwork.**

M.I. Hummel collectibles, which are listed elsewhere in this volume.

The museum address is: Das Berta-Hummel-Museum im Hummelhaus, Strasse 2, D - 84323 Massing, Germany. The museum hours are: 9 a.m. to 5 p.m. Monday through Saturday and 10 a.m. to 5 p.m. Sunday.

The Siessen Convent Hummelsaal (Hall of Hummels)

Sister Maria Innocentia's convent maintains an exhibit of many of her original drawings and paintings. If you are lucky, you may be able to see her renderings of the Stations of the Cross in the adjacent chapel. A selection of Hummel postcards and small prints is offered for sale. There is also the opportunity to see her final resting place in the convent cemetery. The convent is a regular stop on the annual club-sponsored tours.

The convent is located just 3 kilometers out of Saulgau in southern Germany. The address is Kloster Siessen, D-88348 Saulgau, Germany. The hours of operation are: closed Monday; 2 to 4 p.m. Tuesday through Friday; 10 a.m. to noon and 2 to 4 p.m. Saturday; and 1:30 to 4 p.m. Sunday. It is best to phone ahead in case of religious celebrations or other unscheduled closings.

Chapter Two

Collectors' Guide

Buying and Selling

Finding and Buying M.I. Hummel Collectibles

The single, most important factor in any collecting discipline is knowledge. Before you spend your hard-earned funds to start or expand a collection, it is incumbent upon you to arm yourself with knowledge. If you've bought this book, you have made a good start. Now you must study it, learn from it, and refer to it often when you're on your hunt.

But don't stop there. Later in this book we have included a list of other books and publications dealing with the subject. Some are out of print and no longer readily available, but others are easy to obtain. Get them and study them as well. Be sure you get the latest edition.

In today's market, there are many sources, some quite productive and some not so productive, as is true of any collectibles field. Supply and demand is a very important factor in the world of Hummel collecting. We have been through some extraordinary times. Nearly three decades ago, retailers had a very difficult time obtaining Hummel figurines and plates in any quantity, never had a choice of pieces, and often went for weeks with none in stock. They often had to order an assortment, and there were three monetary levels of assortments. In addition, it was often two to three months between ordering them and taking delivery. This was true for almost every retail Hummel dealer in the country. Although the rule is still generally no choice for the smaller

Sometimes there would be 40 or 50 tables like this at a show, all practically empty by the last day.

dealers, production increases have improved over the years to where the number you have to select from at your local dealer is usually pretty good.

In those years of limited supply, even small dealers saw their shipments gone in days. There was a time in the late-1970s and early 1980s that dealers not only couldn't meet collectors' demands, but kept lists of collectors and what each collector was looking for. The result was most of their stock was presold, and leftovers were sometimes fought over.

The shows and conventions that featured Hummel saw great crowds in those early years of the Hummel popularity surge. Frequently, dealers would literally be cleaned out before half the show was over, leaving booths empty of all but tables and display fixtures. The *Luckey's Hummel® Figurines & Plates Identification and Price Guide* was snatched up at one show so fast that the author had none to sell after the first day.

Our economic times have changed all that, but the good news is that collectors now have many sources from which to choose. This is particularly true if you are not specializing in the older trademark pieces. These can be readily found in gift shops, jewelry stores, galleries, and shops specializing in collectibles. Even the popular new television shopping programs feature Hummel figurine sales from time to time. They are also available by mail-order from various dealers around the country, many of whom also deal in the old trademark pieces.

A great way to find them is by looking in the various antique and collectible publications (names and addresses of these are listed elsewhere in the book). Many of them have a classified ad section where dealers and collectors alike offer Hummel figurines and related pieces such as plates.

Productive sources, if you can get to them, are the large annual gatherings of dealers and collectors held around the country. Especially if you're trying to find the older-marked pieces, these shows can be a goldmine. But even if you're a collector of the new pieces, attending the shows is fun and a good learning experience. They usually offer lectures and seminars by experts and dealers, all of whom are subject to much "brain-picking" by crowds of collectors. You also have the opportunity to meet other collectors and learn from them. Just be sure to pick the ones with this book under their arm: they are obviously the smartest!

Of course, the age of technology has brought forth another new venue for finding and selling pieces. The Internet has provided collectors of all sorts of Hummel-related pieces with a place not only to shop, but also to interact in chat rooms or online discussion panels with other collectors. There are even appraisal services on the 'Net where trained appraisers can give you a value to your collection for a fee.

Using the Internet, the possibilities for expanding a collection (or selling one) now seem endless. Take, for example, the number of Hummel-related collectibles on auction Web sites; on eBay.com, a search under the word "Hummel" will bring forth an average of more than 100,000 choices every day. The one caution about using the Internet for buying, however, is to beware of potential fraud. Without the opportunity to actually pick up and inspect a piece, it is sometimes difficult to legitimize authenticity. See "More About E-Buying" for a bit more detail on Internet buying.

Other than at shows, by mail-order, or on the 'Net, you can find old trademark pieces in those shops that sell both new and old pieces. There are a few around the country. With the increased awareness of the value of the older-marked pieces, it is very unlikely—but still possible—that some smaller, uninformed shops could have a few pieces bearing older trademarks, bought some years ago for sale at whatever the current retail price is for the newer ones.

Bargains? Yes, there are bargains to be found. Sometimes you get lucky at auctions if no one else is looking for the particular figurine you have picked out. That would be a rare occurrence at an all-Hummel auction. Estate auctions and sales and country auctions would be your best bet. Flea markets (especially in Europe), junk shops, attics, basements, relatives, friends, acquaintances, and neighbors are by far the best sources for bargains. In short, anywhere one might find curious old gifts, castaways, etc.

These engaging little figurines have, for about 70 years now, been considered a wonderful gift or souvenir. There are so many motifs that you can almost always find one that fits a friend's or relative's particular personality, profession, or avocation. Until recently, they were also relatively inexpensive. So "bone up," and start looking and asking. You may find a real treasure.

More About E-Buying

People today are flocking to online Internet sites to shop for a wide array of collectibles. As more opportunities develop for making the best deal, collectors need to educate themselves on the proper methods of buying online, and by doing so, reduce the risk of possible abuse by an unscrupulous merchant.

When looking to buy Hummels to start a new collection, it's a good idea to start with your local retailer. Not only will retailers carry the latest releases, but they often are aware of other collectors in the area and can perhaps direct you to someone who would be willing to sell some of the rarer pieces on the secondary market.

In 1999, auction sales amounted to $2 billion, and the figures continued to grow into the new century. Although online auctions have tapered somewhat in today's tough economy, I interviewed Federal Trade Commission staff attorney Lisa Hone for the April 2000 edition of *Collector's Mart* magazine and quoted her as saying auctions are popular because they give buyers and sellers wonderful opportunities to find each other.

"If I'm in Alaska, I can reach out all over the world and find a particular piece of Mission furniture or even a Beanie Baby," Hone said. "The vast majority of the times, it works out fine."

In the first half of 1998, the FTC's Bureau of Consumer Protection received about 300 complaints involving online auction fraud, according to Hone. In the first half of 1999, about 6000 such complaints were recorded. The growth of exploitation is not surprising, given the phenomenal expansion of one-on-one trading through the Internet.

Collectors need to be aware of potential risks and apply a full measure of common sense precautions to ensure the safety and reliability of any transaction. Some test of basic principles must be utilized: What is the seller's reputation? Is the seller willing to give me a valid street address where I can find him should something go wrong?

Do I get a warranty? Do I have return privileges?

In order to finesse your collectibles buying online, review the "E-Buying Tips" below for important considerations when you are shopping the 'Net.

With a few common sense precautions, you should be ready to e-shop until your fingers drop.

E-Buying Tips

- Understand how the auction works.
- Check out the seller. For company information, contact the state or local consumer protection agency and Better Business Bureau.
- Be especially careful if the seller is a private individual.
- Get the seller's name, street address, and telephone number to check him/her out or follow up if there is a problem.
- Ask about returns, warranties and service.
- Be wary of claims about collectibles.
- Use common sense and ask yourself: Is this the best way to buy this item? What is the most I am willing to bid?
- Get free insurance through the auction sites whenever possible.
- For assistance, check out these Web sites: www.fraud.com, www.ftc.gov and www. bbbonline.com.

The Price to Pay

The province of this book is primarily Hummel figurines and related articles. The preponderance of these collectibles are made by W. Goebel Porzellanfabrik (hereinafter called Goebel) and most of those covered here bear trademarks other than the one currently being used by the company. It is always nice to have a listing of what is currently being produced by Goebel, along with the suggested retail prices. There is one printed in the back of the book, but a more portable version printed by Goebel should be available at your nearest dealer.

Licenses have been granted to companies other than Goebel to produce various other items. Most, but not all, of these items utilize a two-dimensional Hummel design motif. The first and earliest were those who were licensed to produce prints and postcards. Many companies used these prints by applying them to such things as framed pictures, wall plaques, and music boxes. These and the more recent releases have yet to develop much of a secondary collector market. For this reason, you will see few of them in this book with a quoted collector value.

There are several factors that influence the actual selling price of the old and the new. The suggested retail price list, released by the company periodically, addresses those pieces bearing the current production trademark. Each time the list is released, it reflects changes in the retail price. These changes (usually increases) are due primarily to the basic principle of supply and demand, economic influences of the world money market, ever-increasing material and production costs, the American market demand, and last, but certainly not least, an expanding interest in Germany and the rest of the European market.

The list does not necessarily reflect the actual price you may have to pay. Highly popular pieces in limited supply can go higher and some of the less popular pieces can go for less. This has been the case more in the recent past than now, but the phenomenon still occurs.

The value of Hummel figurines, plates, and other collectibles bearing trademarks other than the one currently being used in production is influenced by some of the same factors discussed earlier, to a greater or lesser extent. The law of supply and demand comes into even more prominent light with regard to pieces bearing the older trademarks, for they are no longer being made and the number on the market is finite. More simply, there are more collectors desiring them than there are available pieces. Generally speaking, the older the trademark, the more valuable or desirable the piece. One must realize, however, that this is not a hard and fast rule. In many instances there are larger numbers available of pieces bearing an older mark than there are of pieces bearing later trademarks. If the latter is a more desirable figure and is in much shorter supply, it is perfectly reasonable for it to be more valuable.

Another factor must be considered. The initial find of the rare International Figurines saw values shoot up as high as $20,000 each. At first, the figurines were thought to exist in just eight designs and in only one or two prototypes of each. Over the years, several more designs and multiples of the figurines have surfaced. Although they are still quite rare, most bring less than half of the original inflated value. So you see, values can fall as the result of an increase in supply of a rare or uncommon piece. This situation can be brought about artificially as well. If someone secretly buys up and hoards a large quantity of a popular piece for a period of time, the short supply will drive the value up. If that supply is suddenly dumped on the market, demand goes down. This has happened more than once in the past, but not so much today.

Yet another circumstance that may influence a fall in pricing is the reissue of a piece previously thought by collectors to be permanently out of production. This has happened because of collectors' past confusion over company terminology with regard to whether a piece was permanently or temporarily withdrawn from production. Many collectors wish to possess a particular item simply because they like it and have no interest in an older trademark version. These collectors will buy the newer piece simply because they can purchase it for less, although recent years have seen the last of the older trademarked pieces go for about the same. It follows naturally that demand for an even older trademark version will lessen under those circumstances.

You may find it surprising that many of the values in the old trademark listing are less than the values reflected in the current Goebel suggested retail price list. You have to realize that serious collectors of old mark Hummel collectibles have very little interest in the price of or the collecting of those pieces currently being produced, except where the list has an influence on the pricing structure of the secondary market. As we have seen, demand softens for some of the later old trademark pieces. That is not to say that those and the current production pieces are not valuable—quite the contrary. They will be collectible on the secondary market eventually. Time must pass. Make no bones about it, with the changing of the trademarks and the passing of time will come the logical step into the secondary market. The principal market for the last two trademarks is found in the general public, not the seasoned collector. The heaviest trading in the collector market in the past couple of years has been in the Crown and Full Bee trademark pieces. The Stylized Bee and Three Line trademark pieces are currently remaining stable and the Last Bee trademark pieces are experiencing a stagnant market.

Selling M.I. Hummel Items

There is an old saying in the antique and collectibles world that goes like this: "You buy at retail and sell at wholesale." Although this is true in some cases, it is most assuredly (and thankfully) not the rule. The axiom can be true if you must sell and the only ready buyer is a dealer whose percent discount equals or exceeds the amount your item has appreciated in value. This can also be true if you have consigned your piece to an auction, although auctions usually allow you to set a reserve. A reserve is the lowest price you will sell at. If bidding doesn't reach your reserve, you still owe the auctioneer his fee, but you get your item back. This is the case whether you are dealing with a traditional auctioneer or an online auction site.

There are several other methods of selling, each of which has its own set of advantages and disadvantages.

Selling to a Dealer

The have-to-sell scenario above is an obvious disadvantage, but selling to a dealer will in most cases, be a painless experience. If you have been fortunate in your acquisitions and the collection has appreciated considerably, it may also be a profitable encounter. If you are not near the dealer and have to ship, then you run the risk of damage or loss.

Running Newspaper Ads

Selling to another collector in your local area is probably one of the easiest and most profitable ways to dispose of your piece(s). There is the advantage of personal examination and no shipping risks.

Running Collector Publication Ads

This is another fine way to get the best price, as long as the sale is to another collector. The same shipping risks exist here also, and you do have to consider the cost of the ad.

Answering Wanted Ads in Collector Publications

The only risk beyond the usual shipping risks is the possibility of the buyer being disappointed and wishing to return the pieces for a refund.

Selling Through a Local Dealer

If you are fortunate enough to have a dealer near you, he/she may take consignments for a percentage.

Selling on the Internet

Although shipping risks and those related to dissatisfied buyers also apply to Internet sales, one advantage over traditional advertisements is not having to pay to publicize your piece (if you have the computer savvy to set up your own Web site). Web sites also offer an opportunity to showcase not only the basic description of a piece, but also a display of a photo of it.

If you are not so technologically advanced that you can run your own Web site, selling via auction Web sites is relatively inexpensive as well. Such Web sites also offer a wide range of services, most notably for billing, which helps the seller lessen his/her risks of a fraudulent sale (buyers using bad checks, stolen credit cards, etc.).

Another advantage to selling on the Internet involves the Web's far-reaching capabilities. It is not called the World Wide Web for nothing! While some collector publications may only be accessible to people living in the United States, for example, the Internet provides worldwide exposure.

Utilize Collector Club Services

The Hummel Collector's Club, Inc. publishes a quarterly newsletter in which it runs sales and wanted ads, free of charge to members. You respond to these ads by mailing your response to the club. They then forward the response, unopened, to the individuals running the ad. The address for membership is Hummel Collector's Club, P.O. Box 257, Yardley, PA 19067-2857. If you need a membership application, write to them or call toll-free at (888) 548-6635.

Possible Pitfalls

The determination of the authenticity of the piece in question is fairly easy in the greatest majority of instances. If you have no reason to suspect the piece of being a fake or forgery and it somewhere bears the incised M.I. Hummel signature, it is probably genuine. In a few instances, the pieces were simply too small for the incised signature to be placed on them without defacing them. Under these circumstances, the company usually places a paper or foil sticker where it is least obtrusive. Often these are lost from the piece over the years, but these small items are few in number and usually readily identifiable by the use of the incised mold number and trademark.

By carefully studying the section on how Goebel utilizes mold numbers on the M.I. Hummel pieces, you will gain much more insight into correct identification.

Be ever-alert to the trademarks found on pieces and how to interpret them (see trademark information later in this chapter). It is a complicated and sometimes confusing system, and you must know how marks are used and what they mean in order to know what you are buying.

Variations are rampant (see individual listings) in both size, coloration, and mold, and you may think you are buying one thing when you're actually getting something quite different.

When it comes to determining the value of broken but expertly restored pieces, they are generally worth one-half or less than the current value of the unbroken "mint" pieces. This value is entirely dependent upon the availability of unbroken mint pieces bearing the same mold number, size designator, and trademark. In the case of a rare piece, however, it is often worth almost as much as the mint piece if expertly restored, due simply to its scarcity. (See the list of restorers in "Care, Protection, and Display.")

Crazing is another important factor to keep in mind. Please refer to "Care, Protection, and Display" for further discussion of this matter.

Detecting Restored Pieces

It is sometimes difficult—or impossible—for the average collector to detect an expert restoration of a Hummel figurine or article. The two most reliable methods are: 1) examination by long-wave ultraviolet light, and 2) examination by X-ray. Until very recently, one could rely almost 100 percent on ultraviolet light examination, but some restorative techniques have been developed in the past few years that are undetectable except by X-ray examination.

Examination by X-ray

Access to X-ray equipment might prove difficult. If you have a good friend who is a doctor or dentist with his/her own equipment, you might be able to get your X-ray by reimbursing expenses. A crack otherwise invisible to the naked eye may appear where the piece has been restored. If the piece does exhibit such a feature, it is safe to assume it is a restored piece. There are some restoration marks, however, that may not show up, so the X-ray examination is not foolproof. The latter represents state-of-the-art restoration.

Examination by Ultraviolet Light

When an undamaged piece is exposed to long-wave ultraviolet light, it will appear uniformly light purple in color; the value of the purple will vary with color on the piece. A crack or fracture with glue in it will appear a lighter color (usually orange or pink), patches will appear almost white, and most new paint will appear a much, much darker purple.

Non-Hummel Items by Goebel

You need to be aware that from 1871, when the company was founded, until 1991, Goebel used the same trademarking system on just about all of its products. In 1991, the company changed the system so that now there is a special trademark that

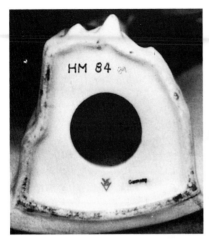

Base marking found on a non-Hummel Madonna made by Goebel. Note the "HM" letter prefix (enhanced here for reproduction with pen and ink).

is used exclusively on M.I. Hummel items. The older Goebel trademark found on an item is, therefore, not necessarily an indication that it is a Hummel design, only that it might be. For further identification, use the guidelines described earlier in this chapter.

You would not believe how many experts receive inquiries from folks who think they have a rare Hummel item only to find that they have another of Goebel's many other products.

With Goebel's M.I. Hummel products, it is the rule that letter prefixes are not used. When a letter or

The Seven Dwarfs from the Walt Disney series by Goebel called Snow White and the Seven Dwarfs. They bear various trademarks from Stylized (TMK-3) through the Last Bee (TMK-5) and measure from 2-3/4" to 3".

letters are used, they are almost invariably a suffix, placed after the incised mold number.

When Goebel marks a non-Hummel item, the mold number usually has a one-, two-, or three-letter prefix associated. Following are a few examples of the many prefixes and what they mean:

- Byj ... Taken from designs by Charlot Byj.
- Dis ... Taken from Walt Disney characters.

A Norman Rockwell piece from Goebel. It bears the "ROCK 217" mold number, the Three Line Mark (TMK-4), and measures 3-5/8" x 5-1/2".

- FF ... Freestanding figure.
- HM ... Madonna.
- HX ... Religious figurine.
- KF ... Whimsical figure.
- Rob ... Taken from designs by Janet Robson.
- Spo ... Taken from designs by Maria Spotl.

There are many more prefix examples than listed here, and the pieces are just as well-made as are the Hummel items and are themselves eminently collectible. They are not Hummel art, however, so be sure before you buy.

There seems to be a developing market for some non-Hummel Goebel products, such as the Charlot Byj "Red Heads" (as they are known) and the Little Monk or "Friar Tuck" pieces. There is already a well-developed secondary market for the Norman Rockwell and Walt Disney character figurines.

Fakes, Forgeries, Imitations, and Copies

Fakes and Forgeries

Though not widespread in number, there have been a few rather obvious alterations to the trademarks and to the figurines themselves, making them appear older or different from the norm and therefore more valuable. There have been additions or deletions of small parts (i.e. birds, flowers, etc.) to figures. Worse, one or two unscrupulous individuals have been reglazing colored figurines and other articles with a white overglaze to make them appear to be the relatively uncommon to rare all-white pieces. The serious collector can sometimes detect these imposters, but it is best left to the experts.

Display plaque for the Goebel Friar Tuck series. The mold number "WZ 2" is incised and inked in, indicating it is a Mother Mold piece. It bears the Stylized Bee (TMK-3), a 1959 copyright date, and measures 4-3/4" x 3-7/8".

This 3" imitation appears to be a combination of *Easter Time* (Hum 384) and *Playmates* (Hum 58). No markings.

Should you purchase a piece that is ultimately proven to be one of these fakes, any reputable dealer would replace your figurine if possible. At the very least, the dealer would refund your money.

Imitations, Copies, and Reproductions of Original Hummel Pieces

Anyone interested in copies should consult the excellent book *Hummel Copycats* by Lawrence L. Wonsch. Wonsch shows that the collecting of copycat M.I. Hummels can be fascinating and fun.

There are many reproductions and imitations of the original Hummel pieces, some better than others, but so far, all are easily detectable upon the most casual examination if one is reasonably knowledgeable about what constitutes an original.

The most common of these imitations are those produced in Japan. They are similar in design motif but obviously not original when one applies the simplest of rules. See explanation of trademarks later in this chapter.

Take note of the photo of *Retreat to Safety* (Hum 201) appearing on page 51. To look at the photo is disconcerting because the figure appears to be genuine. When you hold this particular copy in your hand, however, it feels very light and is obviously inferior. If you look beneath the base, there is the

Plastic imitations of Hum 197, *Be Patient*. A variation with articulation arms is rather uncommon.

Plastic imitation of Hum 201, *Retreat to Safety*. Made in Hong Kong, it appears the mold for this piece was taken directly from a geniune Hummel figurine.

phrase "Made in Hong Kong." Carl Luckey purchased this plastic copy in a truck stop gift shop in a Midwestern state in 1979 for $3.95. It was probably worth about 50 cents at the time. Over the years, many others have surfaced. In fact, there is a whole series of these plastic copies.

These two 4-1/4" figures replicating *Apple Tree Boy* and *Apple Tree Girl* are made of plastic and are decidedly inferior. No markings found.

A 7" imitation of Hum 5, *Strolling Along*.

Many other figurines and articles make obvious attempts at copying the exact design of the genuine article. In every single instance, the falseness becomes immediately detectable as being made of materials and paints severely inferior to the quality exhibited by the real thing. Most are manufactured from a material similar to the plaster or plaster-like substance used in the manufacture of the various prizes one wins at the carnival game booth. Some of these actually bear a sticker proclaiming that they are genuine, authentic, or original Hummel pieces.

The Dubler Figures

During World War II, the Nazi government did not allow the Goebel company to carry on production of Hummel figurines. At that time, a New York firm known as Ars Sacra (a subsidiary of today's Ars Edition in Munich) produced a small collection

AUTHENTIC
HUMMEL FIGURE
PRODUCED BY ARS SACRA
MADE IN USA

Reproduction of ARS SACRA sticker.

of figurines very much like the original designs and others in the Hummel style, but not copying any particular design. Those that were Hummel copies usually bore a 5/8" x 1" foil sticker, as reproduced here. They often also had "B. Hummel" and either "ARS SACRA" or "Herbert Dubler, Inc." associated with the signature. Either version was usually incised into the top or side of the base of the figurine. Frequently a copyright date also appears in the same area. In Wonsh's guide, *Hummel Copycats*, more than

Six Herbert Dubler figurines.

Large and heavy bronze figures on marble.
The one on the left measures 7" and the other 6-1/2".
Incised at the rear of the figures is "Copyright
1942 Herbert Dubler, Inc."

20 of these Dubler figures are pictured. His research indicates the possibility that 61 of these figures were designed and perhaps made.

Most Dubler pieces were made of a chalk-like or plaster of Paris-type substance, but a few were rendered in bronze, and some have even been found cast in silver. The Crestwick Company of New York ostensibly distributed them in the United States.

These rather pitiful Hummel-like figures bear the inscription "Copyright 1947 Decorative Figurines Corp., the Dubler company."

Crestwick later became Hummelwerk, an old U.S. distributing company owned by Goebel. It eventually evolved to the present Goebel operations in the U.S.

Another name associated with Dubler was "Decorative Figurines, Inc." These figurines, also made of plaster of Paris, were almost exact copies.

The English or Beswick Pieces

These interesting pieces are intriguing in that some mystery surrounds their origin. Collectors usually know them together as "The English Pieces." There has been speculation in the past that they have some claim to legitimacy, but there has never been any hard evidence found to support that notion. The backstamp "BESWICK-ENGLAND" indicates they were made by an old and respected English porcelain manufacturer that was later bought

 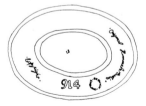

English/Beswick backstamp.

English/Beswick *Strolling Along* (906).

English/Beswick *Shepherd's Boy* (914).

out by Royal Doulton. Royal Doulton finds no reference to the pieces in what records of Beswick were obtained when they bought the company.

There have been 12 different designs identified with or without the Beswick backstamp, M.I. Hummel incised signature, and other markings. The mold numbers are 903 through 914. The number 907 model has never been found. The list follows:

- 903 *Trumpet Boy*
- 904 *Book Worm*

English/Beswick pieces. Left to right with their incised mold numbers: *Meditation* (910), *Trumpet Boy* (903), and *Puppy Love* (909).

English/Beswick *Farm Boy* (912).

- 905 *Goose Girl*
- 906 *Strolling Along*
- 907 (No known name)
- 908 *Stormy Weather*
- 909 *Puppy Love*
- 910 *Meditation*
- 911 *Max and Moritz*
- 912 *Farm Boy*
- 913 *Globe Trotter*
- 914 *Shepherd's Boy*

The figurines are shiny and brightly colored in the faience tradition. Most of them bear the inscription "Original Hummel Studios Copyright" in script letters and some version of the Beswick backstamp. Most, but not all, also bear an incised M.I. Hummel signature along with the base inscriptions described above, and there have been some found with no markings at all. All are sought eagerly by many serious collectors. The collector value range of those bearing the signature is $900-$1200.

Understanding Trademarks

Since 1935, there have been several changes in the trademarks used by Goebel on M.I. Hummel items. In later years of production, each new trademark design merely replaced the old one, but in the earlier years, frequently the new design trademark would be placed on a figurine that already bore the older style trademark. In some cases, a change from an incised trademark to a surface stamped version of the same mark would result in both appearing on the figure. The former represents a transition period from older to newer, and the latter resulted in what are called "Double Crown." This section is meant to give you an illustrated guide to the major trademarks and their evolution to the trademark presently used on Goebel-produced M.I. Hummel items.

Many subtle differences will not be covered because they serve no significant purpose in identifying the era in which an item was produced. There are, however, a few that do help to date

M.J. Hummel © Ꝩ

The Hummel signature as a base rim marking.

MADE IN U.S. ZONE

Made in
U.S.-Zone
Germany.

U.S. Zone

Germany.

U.S.-Zone
Germany.

U.S.-Zone
Germany

U.S. Zone
Germany.

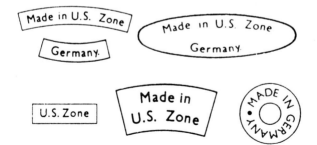

Made in U.S. Zone

Germany.

Made in U.S. Zone
Germany.

U.S. Zone

Made in
U.S. Zone

MADE IN GERMANY

Various base markings from the 1940s.

a piece. These will be discussed and illustrated. The dates of the early trademark changes are approximate in some cases, but probably accurate to within five years or so. Please bear in mind that the dates, although mostly derived from company records, are not necessarily as definite as they appear. There are documented examples where pieces vary from the stated years, both earlier and later. A number of words and phrases associated with various trademarks can, in some cases, help to date a piece.

Note: It is imperative that you understand that the various trademarks illustrated and discussed here have been used by Goebel on all of its products, not just Hummel items, until about mid-1991, when a new mark was developed exclusively for use on M.I. Hummel items.

The Crown Mark (TMK-1): 1934-1950

The Crown Mark (TMK-1 or CM), sometimes referred to as the "Crown-WG," was used by Goebel on all of its products in 1935, when M.I. Hummel figurines were first made commercially available. Subtle variations have been noted, but the illustration at right is all you need to identify

Incised Crown Mark

Stamped Crown Mark

Wide Ducal Crown Mark

the trademark. Those subtle differences are of no important significance to the collector. The letters WG below the crown in the mark are the initials of William Goebel, one of the founders of the company. The crown signifies his loyalty to the imperial family of Germany at the time of the mark's design, around 1900. The mark is sometimes found in an incised circle.

Another Crown-type mark is sometimes confusing to collectors; some refer to it as the "Narrow Crown" and others the "Wide Ducal Crown." This mark was introduced by Goebel in 1937 and used on many of its products. Goebel calls it the Wide Ducal Crown mark, so we shall adopt this name as well to alleviate confusion. To date, most dealers and collectors have thought this mark was never found on a M.I. Hummel piece. Goebel, however, in its newsletter Insights (Vol. 14, No. 3, pg. 8) states that the mark was used "...rarely on figurines," so we will defer to the company and assume there might be some out there somewhere.

Often, as stated earlier, the Crown Mark will appear twice on the same piece, more often one

The base of Hum 163 illustrating the incised Crown Mark and the stamped Full Bee trademark. Note also the use of the decimal designator with the incised mold number.

mark incised and the other stamped. This is, as we know, the "Double Crown."

When World War II ended and the United States Occupation Forces allowed Goebel to begin exporting, the pieces were marked as having been made in the occupied zone. The various forms and phrases to be found in this regard are illustrated below.

These marks were applied to the bases of the figurines, along with the other markings, from 1946 through 1948. They were sometimes applied under the glaze and often over the glaze. The latter were easily lost over the years through wear and cleaning if the owner was not careful. Between 1948 and 1949, the U.S. Zone mark requirement was dropped, and the word "Germany" took its place. With the partitioning of Germany into East and West, "W. Germany," "West Germany," or "Western Germany" began to appear most of the time instead.

Until the early 1950s the company occasionally used a WG or a WG to the right of the incised M.I. Hummel signature. When found, the signature is usually placed on the edge of, or the vertical edge of, the base. Some have been known to confuse this with the Crown Mark (TMK-1) when in fact it is not.

The Full Bee Mark (TMK-2): 1940-1959

In 1950, the Goebel company made a major change in its trademark. The company incorporated a bee in a V. It is thought that the bumblebee part

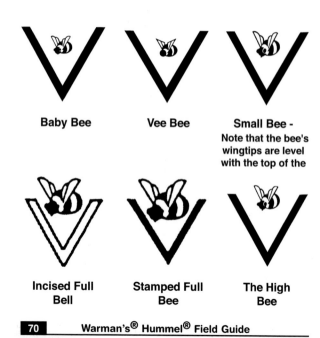

Baby Bee

Vee Bee

Small Bee -
Note that the bee's wingtips are level with the top of the

Incised Full Bell

Stamped Full Bee

The High Bee

of the mark was derived from a childhood nickname of Sister Maria Innocentia Hummel, meaning bumblebee. The bee flies within a V, which is the first letter of the German word for distributing company, Verkaufsgesellschaft. The mark was to honor M.I. Hummel, who died in 1946.

There are actually 12 variations of the Bee marks to be found on Goebel-produced M.I. Hummel items, but some are grouped together, as the differences between them are not considered particularly significant. They will be detailed as a matter of interest.

The Full Bee mark, also referred to as TMK-2 or abbreviated FB, is the first of the Bee marks to appear. The mark evolved over almost 20 years until the company began to modernize it. It is sometimes found in an incised circle. The history of the transition and illustrations of each major change follows. Each of them is still considered to be the Full Bee (TMK-2).

The very large bee flying in the V remained until around 1956, when the bee was reduced in size and lowered into the V. It can be found incised, stamped in black, or stamped in blue, in that order, through its evolution.

The Stylized Bee (TMK-3): 1958-1972

A major change in the way the bee is rendered in the trademark made its appearance in 1960. The Stylized Bee (TMK-3), sometimes abbreviated as Sty-Bee when written, as the major component of the trademark appeared in three basic forms through 1972. The first two are both classified as the Stylized Bee (TMK-3), but the third is considered a fourth step in the evolution, the Three Line Mark (TMK-4). It might interest you to know that Goebel reused the Crown-WG backstamp from 1969 until 1972. It is not always there, but when it shows, it is a small blue decal application. This was done to protect Geobel's copyright of the mark. It otherwise would have run out.

The Large Stylized Bee: This trademark was used primarily from 1960 through 1963. Notice in the illustration that the "W. Germany" is placed to the right of the bottom of the V. The color of the mark will be black or blue. It is sometimes found

Large Stylized Bee

inside an incised circle. When you find the Large Stylized Bee mark, you will normally find a stamped "West" or "Western Germany" in black elsewhere on the base, but not always.

The Small Stylized Bee: This mark is also considered to be TMK-3. It was used concurrently with the Large Stylized Bee from about 1960 and continued in this use until about 1972. Note in the illustration that the "W. Germany" appears centered beneath the V and bee. The mark is usually rendered in blue, and it too is often accompanied by a stamped black "West" or "Western Germany." Collectors and dealers sometimes refer to the mark as the One Line Mark.

W. Germany

Small Stylized Bee

The Three Line Mark (TMK-4): 1964-1972

This trademark is sometimes abbreviated 3-line or 3LM in print. The trademark used the same stylized V and bee as the others, but also included three lines of

Three Line Mark

wording beside it, as you can see. This major change appeared in blue color.

The Last Bee Mark (TMK-5): 1972-1979

Actually developed and occasionally used as early as 1970, this major change was known by some collectors as the Last Bee Mark because the next change in the trademark no longer incorporated any form of the V and the bee. However, with the reinstatement of a bee in TMK-8 with the turn of the new century, TMK-5 is not technically the "Last Bee" any longer. The mark was used until about mid-1979, when Goebel began to phase it out, completing the

Last Bee Mark

transition to the new trademark in 1980. There are three minor variations in the mark shown in the illustration. Generally, the mark was placed under the glaze from 1972 through 1976 and is found placed over the glaze from 1976 through 1979.

The Missing Bee Mark (TMK 6): 1979-1991

The transition to this trademark began in 1979 and was complete by mid-1980. As you can see, Goebel removed the V and bee from the mark altogether.

Missing Bee Mark

Many dealers and collectors lamented the passing of the traditional stylized V and bee, and for a while, called the mark the Missing Bee. In conjunction with this change, the company instituted the practice of adding to the traditional artist's mark the date the artist finished painting the piece. Because the white overglaze pieces are not usually painted, it would be reasonable to assume that the date is omitted on them.

The Hummel Mark (TMK-7): 1991-1999

In 1991, Goebel made a move of historical importance. The company changed the trademark once again. This time, the change was not only symbolic of the reunification of the two Germanies by removal

Hummel Mark

of the "West" from the mark, but very significant in another way. Until then, Goebel used the same trademark on virtually all of its products. The mark illustrated here was for exclusive use on Goebel products made from the paintings and drawings of M.I. Hummel.

The Millennium Bee (TMK-8): 2000-Present

Goebel decided to celebrate the beginning of a new century with a revival in a bee-adorned trademark. Seeking once again to honor the memory of Sister Maria

Millennium Bee Mark

Innocentia Hummel, a bumblebee, this time flying solo without the V, was reinstated into the mark in 2000 and continues today.

Other Base Marks

There are marks in addition to the U.S. Zone marks already covered that can be found on the bases and backs of Goebel Hummel items.

Anniversary backstamp

W. Goebel mark in script.

Final Issue and First Issue Stamps

First of all, there are several colors of marks that you may encounter. The colors found to date are black, purple, red, brown, green, and blue.

The color blue has been used exclusively since 1972. There also have been several combinations of colors found.

The following list contains various words and marks found associated with the trademarks. There are probably more to be discovered, but these are representative.

- W. Germany - by W. Goebel (in script)
- W. Germany - W. Goebel (in script)
- GERMANY - Copr. W. Goebel
- Germany - by W. Goebel, Oeslau 1957
- WEST GERMANY - *II Gbl. 1948
- West Germany - OCCUPIED GERMANY
- WESTERN GERMANY - Western Germany

First Issue, Final Issue, and 125th Anniversary Backstamps

Starting in 1990, Goebel began stamping any newly issued piece with the words "First Issue," during the first year of production only. In 1991, the company began doing the same thing during the last year before retiring a piece, by marking each with the words "Final Issue." The words are also accompanied by the appropriate year date. The stamps are illustrated for you here. The first piece to bear the Final Issue backstamp was Hum 203, *Signs of Spring*, in both sizes. The Final Issue pieces will also be sold with a commemorative retirement medallion hung around them.

Goebel's 125th anniversary was in 1996, and all figures produced in that year bear the special backstamp.

Mold Numbers and Size Designators

Mold Numbers

All Goebel-made Hummel items are made by the use of molds and each unique mold is assigned a number. The number is part of the mold and it, along with the size designator, becomes a part of the finished piece. It is generally incised on the underside of the base, but for practical reasons may appear elsewhere on the item.

Until the mid-1980s, it was thought by most collectors that the highest mold number normally used in production was in the mid-400s. Time and extensive research by writers, dealers, and serious collectors revealed, among other things, that the number in the Goebel design pool most likely

Hum No. 16 *Little Hiker,* $140-$700

exceeds 1,000 by a great deal. A large number
of these have not yet been put into production,
and those planned are designated Possible
Future Editions (PFE) by Goebel. A few of these
(presumably in sample form) have somehow
found their way into the collector market, but
the occurrence is exceedingly rare. When a PFE
becomes a production piece, the earlier PFE
example almost always bears an earlier trademark
than the mark found on the production piece. It,
therefore, retains its unique status. Of the remaining
designs, some may be PFEs and some may never
make it into the collection. The highest mold
number used to date is 2200 for a regular figurine,
but there are many gaps in numerical sequence
and not every number between 1 and 2200 is
currently designated for a figurine now or in the
future. Additionally, there are several ball ornaments
not produced by Goebel that have Hum numbers
ranging from 3012 on up to 3021.

   Note: Before we get into the explanation of the
mold number system, let's eliminate the source of
one area of confusion. Some price lists (including
the one from Goebel) show an odd letter or
number preceded by a slash mark associated with
some Hummel mold numbers. Example: *Flower
Madonna*, 10/l/W. The "W" and the slash are price

list indications that this piece is finished in all white. The actual mold number found incised on the piece is "10/1" only. The "/W," meaning white overglaze finish, and the "/11" or "/6," meaning the normal color finish, are the decor indicators found in some of today's price lists. Remember that they are not part of the mold number itself.

The Size Designator Portion of the Mold Number

While the mold number as discussed earlier in this section was treated as separate from the size designator system, in reality, the two comprise what is sometimes called the Hummel number (Hum number), but more commonly, the mold number. It seems complicated, but isn't really if you factor out Goebel's occasional departure from the rules.

The system has changed little over the years, but has been modified once or twice.

Beginning with the first commercial piece in 1935 and continuing to about 1952, the first size of a particular piece produced was considered by the factory to be the "standard" size. If plans were to produce a smaller or larger version, the factory would place a "0" (zero) or a decimal point after the model or mold number. Frequently, but not always, the "0" would be separated from the mold

Hum No. 1 *Puppy Love,* $305-$1000

number by placing a slash mark (/) between them. There are many cases where the "0" or the decimal point did not appear. Apparently, this signified that at the time, there were no plans to produce other sizes of the same piece.

In the case of Hum 1, *Puppy Love*, there exists only one "standard" size and no size designator has ever been found on the figure. It is reasonable to assume, however, that subsequent changes in production plans would result in other sizes being produced. Therefore, the absence of the "0" or decimal point is not a reliable indicator that there exists only one standard size of the particular piece. In fact, there are some instances where later versions of a piece have been found bearing the "/0," decimal point, and even a "/I," which are smaller than the "standard" for that piece. In some cases, the decimal point appears along with the slash mark. The figurine *Village Boy* (Hum 51), for example, has been seen marked as: "51./0." It could be that when Goebel changed to the slash designator, it just didn't remove the decimal from the mold, but how do you explain the decimal point following the "0"?

The factory used Roman numerals or Arabic numbers in conjunction with the mold numbers to indicate larger or smaller sizes than the standard.

Hum No. 51/3/0 *Village Boy*, $150-$450

The best way for the collector to understand the system is by example. The figure *Village Boy* (Hum 51) has been produced in four different sizes.

Example 51/0: The number 51 tells us that this is the figurine *Village Boy* and the "/0" indicates that it is the first size produced, therefore the standard size. In this case, the size of the piece is roughly 6". The presence of the "/0" (or of a decimal point) is also an indication that the figurine was produced sometime prior to 1952.

As discussed earlier, not all the figures produced before 1952 were designated with the "/0" or decimal point, but if present, it is a great help in beginning to date a figure. The one exception currently known is the discontinuance of the use of the "/0" designator on Hum 353, *Spring Dance*. It was produced with the 353/0 mold and size designator about 1963, taken out of current production later and recently reinstated once more.

By checking the reference for Hum 51, you will note there exist three more sizes: Hum 51/I/0, Hum 51/3/0, and Hum 51/1. Roman numerals are normally used to denote sizes larger than the standard and Arabic numbers indicate sizes smaller than the standard. When utilized in the normal manner, the Arabic number is always found to the left of the "0" designator. There are two exceptions

Hum No. 353/0 *Spring Dance*, $395-$5000

to this norm: one specific, the other general. The specific known exception is *Heavenly Angel*, Hum 21/0/1/2. This is one of only two known instances of the use of a fractional size designator. The last two numbers are incised and read as one-half (1/2). The general exception is the occasional use of an Arabic number in the same manner as the Roman numeral. The Roman numeral size indicator is never used with the "0" designator present, and the Arabic number is never normally used without the "0" designator. Therefore, if you were to find a mold number 51/2, you would know to read it 51/II, and that it represents a piece larger than the standard.

Note: After the mold for Hum 218 (*Birthday Serenade*), the use of the "/0" size designator was eliminated. The mold number (51/II) does not exist. It is used here for illustrative purposes only.

Example 51/1

As before, the number 51 identifies the piece for us. The addition of the "/1" tells us that this is a larger figure than the standard. In this case, it is about 1" larger.

Example 51/2/0 and 51/3/0

Once again, we know the identity of the piece is Hum 51, *Village Boy*. In both cases, there is an Arabic number, the mold number, and the "/0," therefore we can assume both are smaller than the standard. The 51/2/0 is smaller than 5" and the 51/3/0 is even smaller still.

The "0" and decimal point size designators are no longer in use. Keeping in mind the cited exceptions, we can usually assume that a figure with the mold number and no accompanying Arabic or Roman numerals is the standard size for that model. If the mold number is accompanied by Roman numerals the figure is a larger size, ascending to larger sizes the higher the numeral.

There seems to be no set standard size or set increase in size for each of the Arabic or Roman numeral size designators used in the collection. The designators are individually specific to each model and bear no relation to the designators on other models.

Additional Designators

There are a number of pieces in the collection—table lamps, candy boxes, bookends, ashtrays, fonts, plaques, music boxes, candleholders, plates, and sets of figures—that may have additional or different designators. A list follows, with explanations of how each is marked.

Table Lamps are numbered in the traditional manner. Some later price lists show the number preceded by an "M." Example: M/285.

Chick Girl candy box (Hum III/57).

Candy Boxes (Candy Bowls) are covered cylindrical deep bowls, the cover being topped with one of the Hummel figures. They are numbered with the appropriate mold number for the figure and preceded with the Roman numeral "III." Example: "III/57" is a candy box topped with Hum 57, *Chick Girl.*

Bookends are both large figures with provisions for weighting with sand and smaller figures placed on wooden bookend bases. The only sand-weighted bookends are the *Book Worms.* The designation for a bookend is accomplished by placing an "A" and "III" after the assigned Hummel mold number for the bookends. Example: Hum 61/A and Hum 61/B are a set of bookends utilizing Hum 58 and Hum 47, *Playmates* and *Chick Girl.* These are the current designations. In some cases if the figurines are removed from the bookend bases they are indistinguishable from a regular figurine.

Ashtrays are numbered in the traditional manner.

Fonts are numbered in the traditional manner. Exception: There is a font, Hum 91 (*Angel at Prayer*), in two versions. One faces left; the other right. They are numbered 91/A and 91/B respectively.

Plaques are numbered in the traditional manner.

Music Boxes are round wooden containers in which there is a music box movement, topped

Hum 61/A and Hum 61/B: A set of bookends that utilizes the figurines *Playmates* (Hum 58) and *Chick Girl* (Hum 47) as part of their design.

with a traditional Hummel model that rotates as the music plays. The catalog and price list number for the music box is the Hummel number for the piece on the box followed by the letter "M." If the figure is removed from the top it will not have the "M" but will be marked in the traditional manner.

Candleholders are numbered in the traditional manner. They sometimes have Roman numerals to the left of the model designator in price lists. These indicate candle size: I = 0.6 cm, II = 1 cm.

Plates are numbered in the traditional manner. To date, none have been produced with the size designator, only the mold number.

Sets of figures are numbered with one model number sequence and followed by the designation /A, /B, /C ... /Z, to indicate each figure is part of one set. Example: The *Nativity Set* 214 contains 15 Hummel figures, numbers 214/A, 214/B, 214/C, and so on. In the case of Nativity Sets there are some letters that are not used. The letters "I" and "O" are not utilized because of the possibility of confusing them with the Roman numeral "I" or Arabic "I" and "0."

Additional Notes on Special Markings

Sets

Any time there have been two or more pieces in the collection that were meant to be matched as a pair or set, the alphabetical listings A through Z are respectively applied to the Hummel mold numbers in some way. Exception: Sometimes called the *"Little Band"* are the three figures: Hum 389, Hum 390, and Hum 391. They do not bear the A, B, C designating them as a set. The piece actually entitled

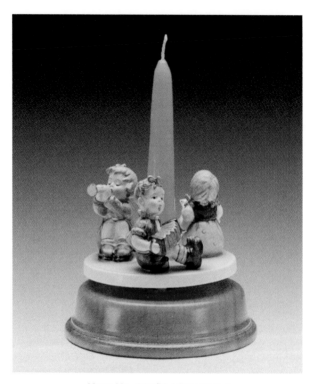

Hum No. 388/M *Little Band*
(candle holder and music box) $400-$500

"*Little Band*" is Hum 392, an incorporation of these three figures on one base together. References to the "*Little Band*" and the "*Eight-Piece Orchestra*" are occasionally found in price lists that include Hummel numbers 2/0, 1/I, 89/I, 89/II, 129, 389, 390, and 391. It's a charming group, but not officially a set.

Copyright Dates

The year date incised on the base of many M.I. Hummel pieces is the source of much confusion to some collectors. The year date is the copyright date. The copyright date is the date the original mold for that particular piece was made and not the date the

Example of a copyright.

piece was made. It bears no relationship whatsoever with the date of making the item, only the mold. As a matter of fact, there are many molds that are years old and still being used to make figures today. The copyright date doesn't always appear on the older pieces, but all those currently being made will have it.

The Making of M.I. Hummel Figurines and Plates by Goebel

The question most asked by those uninitiated to the Hummel world is: "Why do they cost so much?" It is not an unreasonable question, and the answer can be simply that they are handmade. That, however, really doesn't do justice to the true story. The making of Hummel pieces is immensely complex—truly a hand operation from start to finish. The process requires no less than 700 steps! Those few of you who have been fortunate enough to visit Goebel's northern Bavaria facility know how complicated the operation is. Others of you who have seen the Goebel film and/or visited the facsimile factory on its 1985 U.S. tour have a pretty good idea.

To call the facility a factory is misleading, for the word "factory" causes the majority of us to conjure up an image of machinery and automated assembly

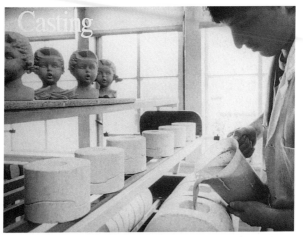

Pouring the slip into the mold.

lines. It is not that at all. It is an enormous artists'
and artisans' studio and workshop complete with
friendly relaxed surroundings, including good music,
hanging baskets, and potted plants. In short, it is a
pleasant place to create and work. It is packed with
highly trained and skilled artists and craftspeople.
Each of them must undergo a full three-year
apprenticeship before actually taking part in the
fashioning of the figurines and other items that are

Refining the assembled pieces prior to the first firing.

made available to the collector. This apprenticeship is required no matter whether the worker is a mold-maker or painter. Each specialist in the process must understand the duties of the others.

There is insufficient space to elaborate on all 700 steps involved, so they have been grouped into six basic areas: Sculpting the Master Model, Mother or Master Mold-Making, Molding the Pieces, Bisque Firing, Glaze Firing, and Painting and Decorating (décor firing).

1. Sculpting the Master Model

It is estimated that there are 1,200 to 1,500 M.I. Hummel artworks from which Goebel may choose to render into a three-dimensional figurine or other item. Once a piece of art is chosen, a master sculptor fashions a model in a water-based Bavarian black clay. This is a long process during which the artists must not just reproduce the art but interpret it. They must visualize, for instance, what the back of

Master Sculptor Gerhard Skrobek sculpting the figurine *Ring Around the Rosie*, Hum 348.

the piece must look like and sculpt it as they think M.I. Hummel would have rendered it. Once the wax model is deemed acceptable, it is taken to the Siessen Convent, where it is presented for approval or disapproval. If the preliminary model is approved, it is then taken back to Goebel for the next step.

2. Master or Mother Mold-Making

A figurine cannot be made from a single mold because of its complexity. Therefore, after a very careful study of the model, it is strategically cut into several pieces. Some figurines must be cut into as many as 30 pieces for molding. For example, Hum 396 (Ride into Christmas) had to be cut into 12 separate pieces and Hum 47 (Goose Girl) into seven.

Using the Goose Girl's seven pieces, we continue. Each of the seven are placed on a round or oval base and secured with more clay. The base is then surrounded by a piece of flexible plastic that extends above the piece to be molded. Liquid plaster of Paris is then poured into it. The dry plaster of Paris is removed, resulting in an impression of the part. This process must be repeated for the other six parts. After each of the seven parts is molded, the result is 14 separate mold halves. From these, the mother molds (sometimes called the master molds) are made. These are made from an acrylic resin. The mother molds are cream-colored and very durable. It is from the mother molds that the working molds are made. The plaster of Paris working molds can be used only about 20 times, at which time a new set must be made from the mother molds.

Before full production of a new figure is commenced, a few samples are made. The figure must again be carried to the Siessen Convent for approval, rejection, or recommendations for changes. Once final approval is given, the piece is ready for production. That could be immediately or years later.

3. Molding and Assembly

All the pieces in the collection are made of fine earthenware, consisting of a mixture of feldspar, kaolin, and quartz. It is the finest earthenware available. Both porcelain and earthenware come under the definition of ceramic. Add just a bit more kaolin, and the earthenware would become porcelain. Goebel chooses to use earthenware because of its inherent softness. That softness is considered best for Hummel items.

The liquid mixture of the three ingredients plus water is called slip. The slip is poured into the working molds and left for a period of time. The porous character of the plaster of Paris acts like a sponge and draws moisture out of the slip. After a carefully monitored time, the remaining slip is poured out of the mold, leaving a hollow shell of the desired thickness. The parts are removed from the molds and while still damp, they are assembled, using the slip as a sort of glue. The assembled piece is then refined: all seams and imperfections are removed and the more subtle areas are detailed. The piece is then set aside to dry for about a week.

4. The Bisque Firing

Bisque is fired, unglazed ceramic. The dry assembled pieces are gathered together and fired in a kiln for 18 hours at 2,100 degrees Fahrenheit. This results in a white, unglazed bisque figurine.

5. The Glaze Firing

The bisque-fired pieces are then dipped into a tinted glaze mixture. The glaze is tinted to assure that the whole piece is covered with the mixture. The tint is usually green so that any uncovered area will show up white. The dipped pieces are then fired at 1,872 degrees Fahrenheit. When removed from the kiln after cooling, they are a shiny white.

6. The Painting and Decorating

The colors are mixed in small amounts and given to the painters only as needed. Some of the colors

One of the final steps of decorating prior to decor firing.

react to each other upon firing, so oftentimes, the item must be painted with one or a few colors and fired before others can be applied. This results in multiple decor firings before the pieces are finished. In some cases, up to 10 separate firings are required before they are finished and ready for distribution.

As you can see now, the making of the pieces is a long, involved, and painstaking operation. As noted earlier there are 700 separate operations, the workers are highly trained and experienced, and there are 25 different quality-control inspection

Hand-painting a face.

One of the light and cheerful studios where artists paint the figurines.

points. In spite of this, each figure is unique because it is the result of a manual operation. No matter how a piece is assembled or painted, no matter how experienced a worker is, he or she is still a human being, inherently incapable of creating identical copies. That is part of the magic. Each piece is a joy, each unique, each a handmade work of art.

Care, Display, and Protection

Caring for Your Collection

Direct sunlight

The first consideration is the potential damage from direct sunlight. It can wreak havoc on just about any type of collectible, including kiln-fired colors on the pieces and the decals under the glaze. Once this occurs, the damage is irreversible. Some of the older figurines are much more susceptible to this than the newer ones. A few have discolored somewhat due to environmental and atmospheric pollution. In the early years, the pigments used in the paints, while the finest available at the time, were not as durable and lasting as those used today and were more sensitive to the caustic elements of air pollution.

Caring for your collection involves many things, including displaying pieces where they are not susceptible to direct sunlight. The display shown here, although aesthetically pleasing, is perhaps not the best choice as the positioning so close to a window with somewhat sheer curtains may result in an irreversible discoloration of the figurines.

Crazing

Crazing is defined as fine cracks in the glaze of ceramics, normally unintentional, resulting from the unequal shrinking of the glaze and the body of the object. It is manifest as a "crackle-look" finish or a fine, intricate web of what appear to be cracks in the glaze of a ceramic piece. This phenomenon is apparently inherent in the ceramic arts and is most likely to occur in older pieces, but can occur in newer ones as well.

In the introduction of *World Ceramics* (1968, Hamlyn Publishing Group, Ltd.), editor Robert J. Charleston says: "A glaze must be suited to the body of the pot which it covers, or it may crack..." Fired earthenware is quite porous and can absorb moisture if not completely covered by a suitable glaze. It is of paramount importance that the earthenware body and its glaze expand and contract uniformly. If they don't, crazing may result.

In fact, in some circles crazing is accepted as proof of antiquity. Most all ancient Chinese ceramics exhibit crazing. Whether or not crazing deters one from purchasing a piece is really up to the individual collector.

Hum No. 330 *Baking Day*, $250-$5,000

**Hum No. 14/A and 14/B *Book Worms*
(Bookends), $400-$1600**

Some Display Tips to Help Prevent Crazing:
Although no one can guarantee the prevention of
crazing, nor of its reoccurrence after craze reversal,
there are some precautions that you should be
aware of.

- Heat or cold can exacerbate crazing
  tendency, so avoid any circumstances where
  your pieces would be subject to heat or cold
  extremes.
- A sudden change in temperature can also
  make worse the tendency toward crazing.

- Avoid air pollution if possible.
- Avoid excessive handling.
- When cleaning by immersion in water or any other solution, try to prevent entry through airholes. Tape them or otherwise block them. If you do get liquid inside, allow the pieces to air dry for a long time before placing them back on display. Be sure to remove whatever you used to block the airholes.

Cleaning

A simple periodic dusting of earthenware or ceramic pieces is always a good idea, but occasionally, they may need a little freshening up. Through the M.I. Hummel Club, Goebel sells an M.I. Hummel Care Kit that consists of two specially formulated cleaning solutions and some brushes, all designed specifically with earthenware, ceramic, and porcelain collectibles in mind. It also includes an instruction booklet.

Should you not wish to order the kit, you can still clean your items. Use your kitchen sink or a similar large vessel. Line it with a towel or other soft material to minimize the possibility of breakage when handling your figures. Make up a solution of barely warm water and a mild soap, such as baby shampoo. Cover the airhole(s) with tape or by some

To help keep your collectibles looking nice,
dust them regularly, especially when they are
displayed on a table as above. Occasionally, you may
also clean them with a soft toothbrush, mild soap
(baby shampoo, for example), and water. When in
doubt about cleaning, consult an expert.

other method. Dip the piece in the solution and scrub gently with a very soft toothbrush or similar soft-bristle brush, all the while holding it over the towel-lined sink. Rinse it off here also. It may take more than one washing if the piece is heavily soiled. Dab it with a soft, absorbent cloth and place on the same type of surface to air dry. Should you be unable to avoid getting water inside the figure, it may take quite some time to dry out.

Many knowledgeable dealers and collectors use strong detergents without harm, but it's probably best to be reluctant to use them as they may contain chemicals or other harsh additives that could be incompatible with the finish. At the very least, you may lose some of the base markings.

If while handling your figures, you notice a tinkling or rattling sound, don't worry. When the figure is being made sometimes a small piece comes loose inside the figure and rattles around. Sometimes, depending on the shape and design of the figure, you can stop this by injecting a little household glue into the interior of the figure through the airhole(s) and shaking it until the rattle stops. Place it on its side until it dries. Presto! No more rattle.

Cleaning paper collectibles beyond dusting is not recommended. If you are fortunate enough to own an original drawing or painting, proper archival framing and care of the frame is recommended. Best advice? Don't touch it. Leave the cleaning of such things to the professionals.

Displaying Your Collection

The display of your collection is limited only by your imagination. This section is not meant to help you with display ideas, but to give you some practical information and guidance for displaying your collection safely and securely.

One of the first considerations is the strength of the display case, if you choose to go that route. You should be sure that your display unit is strong enough to hold your collection safely. Remember, a large group of earthenware figurines can be very heavy.

Remember also the severe damage that direct sunlight can inflict on just about any type of collectible. Try to avoid displaying on a mantle if there is ever a fire in the fireplace. You can cause severe damage to any framed artwork placed there.

Protecting Your Collection

Safeguards

We have discussed the strength factor with regard to the display fixture. Another consideration should be security. Certainly if there are any innocent—but mischievous—little hands about, keep

Remember that display is only limited by
your imagination. Don't be afraid to mix your
Hummel figurines in with a variety of other
collectibles as shown here.

the displays out of their reach and cabinets latched or locked. The most important consideration should be security. This is especially true if you have a significant and/or large collection.

After you have given the usual attention to normal home security, there are some things you need to consider with respect to your collection. No matter how tempting or flattering, turn down any media attention to your collection. This is a red alert to thieves, and yes, there are Hummel thieves. Most thefts take place from display tables set at shows and vehicles used to transport them to and from such events, but there have been instances of home burglary and armed robbery in the home. Keep knowledge of your collection among family and friends. If you don't have a home security system, consider installing one. Fairly inexpensive do-it-yourself systems have been developed. Some are even wireless, eliminating the need to run wires all over the house. Whether you are handy with this sort of thing, the best route may be a professionally installed system. It's your call.

What To Do When It's Broken

How you react to breakage depends upon the nature of the item and its value, intrinsic or sentimental. If you attach great meaning to the piece, but it is a relatively inexpensive item, you could simply glue it back together. If it has great sentimental value and you have the wherewithal, by all means, have it professionally restored. If you have damaged a very rare or valuable piece, it might be worth having it professionally restored. Restoration can be expensive and take quite some time, so you must first decide whether it is worth the trouble, and more importantly, whether the piece will be worth as much or more than the cost.

There are three types of restoration: cold repairing, firing, and bracing. The method used in the greatest majority of cases where Hummel figures are concerned is cold repairing. Cold repairing is the least expensive of the three, and the results are very good. You will probably not be able to detect the repairs with the naked eye. Examination by X-ray and/or long-wave ultraviolet light is the only way to detect a professionally restored piece of earthenware or porcelain.

In selecting a restorer, a personal visit to the shop is advisable. There, you can look over work that is in process and maybe even see a few finished restorations. Many professionals keep a photo album of their work as well. Ask for some references, get an estimate for the job, and find out how long of a wait there is. In most cases, a long wait (we can be talking months here, folks) means many people on the list, and that is usually an indication of a good reputation. The best way to be sure is to get a recommendation from a friend or trusted dealer.

The following list of general restorers is a combination of the list provided by the M.I. Hummel Club and a list developed over the 25 years this book has existed. It is by no means complete, for there are dozens more around the country doing competent, professional restorations. Over the years, there have been dealers and collectors who have not been satisfied with the work or service of some of them, while on the other hand, there has been praise from others regarding the same restorers. In fairness to all of them, I cannot be responsible for recommendations and therefore offer only the list. The general restorers are listed alphabetically by the state in which they are located.

Restorers

Arizona

CHINA AND CRYSTAL CLINIC
Victor Coleman
1808 North Scottsdale Road
Tempe, AZ 85203
(480) 945-5510
(800) 658-9197

California

ATTIC UNLIMITED
22435 La Palma Avenue
Yorba Linda, CA 92887
(714) 692-2940

CERAMIC RESTORATION
Gene Gomas
Manteca, CA 95336
(209) 823-3922

MARK R. DURBAN
P.O. Box 4084
Big Bear Lake, CA 92315
(714) 585-9989

FOSTER ART RESTORATION
711 West 17th Street
Suite C-12
Costa Mesa, CA 92627
(800) 824-6967

GEPPETTO IMPORTS & RESTORATION
Barry J. Korngiebel
31121 Via Colinas, No. 1003
Westlake Village, CA 91362
(818) 889-0901

HOUSE OF RENEW
27601 Forbes Road, Unit 55
Laguna Niguel, CA 92677
(949) 582-3117

JOAN WALTON
San Diego, CA
(619) 291-6539

JUST ENTERPRISES
2790 Sherwin Avenue, No. 10
Ventura, CA 93003
(805) 644-5837

VENERABLE CLASSICS
645 Fourth Street, Suite 208
Santa Rosa, CA 95404
(707) 575-3626

Colorado

HERBERT F. KLUG CONSERVATION
2270 South Zang Court
Lakewood, CO 80228
(303) 985-9261

Connecticut

WALTER C. KAHN
76 North Sylvan Road
Westport, CT 06880

Florida

ROBERT E. DiCARLO RESTORATION
P.O. Box 616222
Orlando, FL 32861
(407) 886-7423

RESTORATIONS OBJECTS D'ART
Eric W. Idstrom Company
12500 Southeast U.S. Highway 301
Belleview, FL 32620
(352) 245-8862

MAISON GINO, INC.
Ginette or Irving Sultan
2021 North Bay Road
Miami Beach, FL 33140
(305) 532-2015

Illinois

J.B. SERVICES
John and Betty Bazar
2302 Sudbury Lane
Geneva, IL 60134

WAYNE WARNER
Route 16, Box 557
Bloomington, IL 61704
(309) 828-0994

Iowa

MAXINE'S LTD. GIFT GALLERY
7144 University Avenue
Des Moines, IA 50311
(515) 255-3197

Massachusetts

ROSINE GREEN ASSOCIATES
89 School Street

Brookline, MA 02446
(617) 277-8368

SHROPSHIRE GALLERY
J. Kevin Samara
274 South Street
Shrewsbury, MA 01545
(508) 842-5001

SHROPSHIRE GALLERY
600 Main Street
Shrewsbury, MA 01545
(508) 845-6317

New Jersey

BAER SPECIALTY SHOP
259 East Browning Road
Bellmawr, NJ 08031
(856) 931-0696

RESTORATIONS BY VALERIE
Valerie Schleifer
4 Country Club Court
Livingston, NJ 07039
(973) 992-9270
(973) 887-7326
Fax: (973) 992-8509

New York

CHINA AND GLASS REPAIR STUDIOS
282 Main Street
Eastchester, NY 10709
(914) 337-1977

FREDI W. BOESE M.I. HUMMEL RESTORATION
P.O. Box 933
309 Route 17 M
Harriman, NY 10926
(845) 783-4438
www.frediboese.com

IMPERIAL CHINA
22 North Park Avenue
Center, NY 11570
(516) 764-7311

RESTORATIONS UNLIMITED
Donna Curtin
1209 Milton Avenue
Syracuse, NY 13204
(315) 488-7123

CERAMIC RESTORATION OF WESTCHESTER, INC.
Hans-Jurgen Schindhelm
81 Water Street
Ossining, NY 10562
(914) 762-1719

Ohio

COLONIAL HOUSE OF COLLECTIBLES
182 Front Street, Terrace Park
Berea, OH 44017
(440) 826-4169

OLD WORLD RESTORATIONS, INC.
5729 Dragon Way, Suite 6
Cincinnati, OH 45227
(513) 271-5459

WIEBOLD ART CONSERVATION LAB
413 Terrace Place
Cincinnati, OH 45174
(513) 831-2541

Pennsylvania

HARRY A. EBERHARDT AND SON, INC.
2010 Walnut Street
Philadelphia, PA 19103
(215) 568-1877

A. LUDWIG KLEIN AND SONS, INC.
683 Sunnytown Pike
P.O. Box 145
Harleysville, PA 19438
(215) 256-9004

KRAUSE'S
97 West Wheeling Street
Washington, PA 15301
(724) 228-5034

CRAZEMASTERS
c/o Hummel Collectors Club, Inc.
1261 University Drive
Yardley, PA 19067-2857
(215) 493-6204

South Dakota

D & J GLASS CLINIC, INC.
Route 3, Box 330
Sioux Falls, SD 57106
(605) 361-7524

Texas

SHARON LEWIS HOBBY
8902 Deer Haven Road
Austin, TX 78737
(512) 301-2294

Virginia

CLAY WERKS LTD.
4058 Main Street
P.O. Box 353
Exmore, VA 23350
(757) 414-0567

Canada

J&H CHINA REPAIR
8296 Saint George Street
Vancouver, BC
Canada V5X 3S5
(604) 321-1093

ARTWORK RESTORATION
30 Hillhouse Road
Winnipeg, MB
Canada R2V 2V9
(204) 334-7090

CLASSIC ART RESTORATION
1260 Yonge Street
Toronto, ON
Canada M4T 1W5
(416) 968-9000

Insuring and Cataloguing Your Collection

"Insurance after a theft is like taking medicine after death."

This adage speaks pointedly to the problems that can occur when collectors fail to take the time to get their valuable collections properly insured and protected.

I know many collectors who have spent countless hours making weekend trips all over the country in pursuit of special items to add to their collections, yet they have not invested a few hours of time to adequately protect that same collection. Many collectors are also ignorant of the increased replacement value of their entire collection.

Collections by their very nature generally appreciate over time, with the collector not always aware of the inflation factor or the secondary market quotations for the pieces they have acquired. None of us care to dwell on the prospect of having our treasures stolen, broken or lost in transit, but a few logical precautions can properly protect the collection that you have so lovingly assembled.

Take the time necessary to review the options available regarding insurance for your collectibles. Several years of speaking on the subject of appraising and insuring collectibles has made me keenly aware of the lack of experience and understanding among collectors regarding insurance policy options for protecting their valuables.

One of the most important aspects of shopping for a good policy is to make a date with yourself to get the project started and stick to it. Don't procrastinate!

Insurance agents are generally accommodating and eager to help you obtain a good policy to protect your collectibles. Still, the buyer must truly beware.

It is always a good idea to get quotes from two or three different insurance companies because some specialize in certain types of policies. Be sure to find out exactly what is covered in the policy being quoted. For example, will it cover breakage, burglary, loss, damage, fire, etc.?

There are several types of coverage available today: valuable articles coverage (VAC); homeowner's or renter's; a separate endorsement to an existing policy; an endorsement to a business policy; or a completely separate policy.

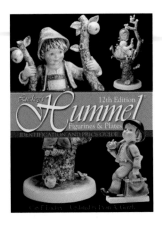

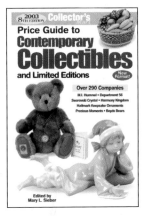

Reliable pricing sources, such as *Collector's Mart Price Guide to Limited Edition Collectibles* or *Luckey's Hummel Figurines & Plates Identification & Price Guide, 12th Edition*, are essential tools when cataloguing your collection for insurance purposes.

Rates for insurance policies vary widely from company to company. Your best bet is to talk with other collectors to find out what companies they have dealt with, how pleased they have been with their coverage, and how their rates compare to what you have been quoted.

Because the insurance sales system works like any other free enterprise, agents are competing with others for your business. They may not want to burden you with too many details about insuring your collection, lest they drive you toward another agency. Therefore, it is up to you, the collector, to retain proper documentation regarding your collection's value.

Insurance agents will usually allow you to place the values on your items by using various reliable publications, such as this book, the *Collector's Mart Price Guide to Limited Edition Collectibles*, the *Collectibles Market Guide & Price Index* by Collector's Information Bureau, or various line-specific editions of *The Greenbook*.

If you already have a homeowner's policy, the best place to begin your insurance search is with your existing agent. Ask him to check your policy's fine print to see if your collection is indeed covered as part of the policy. It is important that you know exactly what is covered and what value will be paid in case you have a claim.

Replacement Value or Fair Market Value

Generally, most collectors will want to insure their collections for "current replacement value." Replacement value is the stated amount that it would take to replace the items if they were damaged, stolen, or lost.

Fair market value is the value of the collection if it were sold suddenly at auction or by any other willing seller/willing buyer arrangement. The fair market value is usually used for reports to the Internal Revenue Service when a collection is donated to a museum or charity. However, some collectors may feel that if their collection were completely lost, current fair market value would make the most sense for a "cash settlement" by the insurance company. A collector of advance years, who may not consider adding to his collection after a loss, may opt for fair market value coverage.

Cataloguing/Documentation

Cataloguing or documentation of your collection is a must when a claim is filed with an insurance company. Here are some possibilities that can make this task much easier.

You can free yourself from the burden of having to complete the documentation of your collection by contracting the services of a professional appraiser.

Two outstanding appraisal organizations exist in the United States with members that are experts in various areas of collectibles: The American Society of Appraisers (ASA), P.O. Box 17265, Washington, DC 20041, and The International Society of Appraisers (ISA), 16040 Christensen Road, Suite 320, Seattle, WA 98188-2929. These organizations can give you the names of experts in various fields of interest in your respective area.

Appraisals

An appraiser is a person who determines the value of an item or items for insurance purposes and supplies the necessary information for the settlement of damage claims. The professional appraiser is also the person who determines the value of the collection at the time it is donated to a tax-exempt institution or charity.

Remember that appraising is not a casual matter. All expert appraisals must be accurate and precise, and should be updated annually to reflect market changes. Often an appraiser must be able to stand up in court if litigation arises from a dispute over valuation of the property.

Select an appraiser in the same manner you would select your family physician or attorney. Don't be afraid to ask for credentials and what type of

experience the individual has acquired. Be careful
not to rely solely on a shop owner purporting to be
an "appraiser." It is also wise to check with collector
friends as to whom they trust and feel confident with
for appraisal opinions.

Choose an appraiser based on these criteria:

- Documented accomplishments (experience)
- Professional certification (education)
- Reputation
- Personal interview (ask for credentials)
- Professional memberships
  (member of ASA or ISA)

Detailed Inventory

Complete a list or cataloguing system of all the
items in your collection. Although some insurance
companies may not request such a list, you should
have an inventory for your own use to determine
your collection's value. With some policies, it may
not be possible to receive reimbursement for the full
value of your collection without a list.

Record the following basic information for
each item:

- Item name
- Series name
- Year of issue
- Artist's name

Hum No. 142/3/0 *Apple Tree Boy*, $180-$550

- Manufacturer's name
- Edition limit/edition number (Hum number)
- Size/dimensions
- Your original cost
- Added expenses (shipping, framing, restoration, etc.)
- Special markings (artist's signatures, etc.)
- Date of purchase
- Secondary market history (if purchased on secondary market)
- Location in your home (for burglary or loss)
- Insurance company/policy or rider number

Record each new item you buy at the time of purchase so as not to get behind on your cataloguing. Make a date with yourself to update this material periodically, possibly after you complete your income taxes for the year. The pleasure of seeing how your collection is growing may offset the chores of preparing tax returns!

Large index cards will handle the pertinent information, or you may prefer to invest in one of the published record books, such as:

- *The Kovels' Organizer for Collectors* by Ralph and Terry Kovel (Crown Publishers, 1 Park Avenue, New York, NY 10016)

- *The Official Collector's Journal* (The House of Collectibles Inc., 201 East 50th Street, New York, NY 10022)
- *Collectors Inventory File* (Collectors News, Grundy Center, IA 50638)

These books may also be available in your local bookstore.

Depending on how technologically advanced you are, you may also develop a cataloguing system on your home computer. There are few software packages available, like The Collectible Dealers FastTrack Inventory and Business Management System 2002 TM available through the Antique and Art Information Network, Inc. Web site at www.aain. com. Though the name of the software makes it sound as though it is exclusive for dealers, it is also useful for individual collector use.

If you prefer not to invest in someone else's software system, it is quite simple to establish your own electronic inventory cataloguing system simply with the help of any spreadsheet program such as Microsoft Excel. Each needed piece of information can be entered into cells with the appropriate column headers, and suddenly you've got a nice electronic catalog.

Photo and Video Documentation

One extra backup to any cataloguing process is to show actual photographs or video of the pieces contained within your collection.

Refer to the special chapter in this book for instructions on photographing your collection. You can take the pictures and attach them to a written description of each piece including trademarks and any other marks found on the base. These will not usually be visible in the photos. Record the exact size and any other characteristic unique to your piece. Some put this information on the back of the photo itself.

If you choose to go the electronic cataloguing route, digital cameras will also allow you to visually inventory your collection and keep the images on a disc. Or, you can take photos the traditional way and scan the images with a computer scanner for storage as digital images on a disc.

A third option for establishing a pictorial record of your collection is to record everything on videotape with a personal camcorder. Begin with a general overview of the entire collection so the viewer can get a feel for its size and where it is displayed. After the introductory shots, detailed looks at each piece constitute a complete video document.

Inventory Safe-Keeping

Whatever method you use to inventory, catalogue, or document your collection, be sure to make a duplicate list, video, set of photographs, compact disc, etc. to be kept in a safe deposit box or some other secure location away from your home or where you keep your collection. You don't want your catalog stolen or burned up with your collection. Your insurance company will very likely require an itemized list with description and value. Your safely stored catalog will be a big help to you and them in the case of a disaster.

Glossary

The following is an alphabetical listing of terms and phrases you will encounter in this book as well as other related books, references, and literature during the course of collecting Hummel items. In some cases, they are specific and unique to Hummel collecting and others are generic in nature, applying to other earthenware, ceramic, and porcelain as well. Refer to this glossary whenever you read or hear something you don't understand. Frequent use of it will enable you to become well versed in collecting Hummel figurines and other related items.

Airholes: Small holes under the arms or other unobtrusive locations to vent the hollow figures during the firing stage of production. This prevents them from exploding as the interior air expands due to intense heat. Many pieces have these tiny little holes, but often they are difficult to locate. Those open at the bottom usually have no need for these holes.

Anniversary Plate: In 1975 a 10" plate bearing the Stormy Weather motif was released. Subsequent anniversary plates were released at five-year intervals. 1985 saw the third and last in the series released.

Annual Plate: Beginning in 1971, the W. Goebel firm began producing an annual Hummel plate. Each plate contains a bas-relief reproducing one of the Hummel motifs. The first was originally released to the Goebel factory workers in 1971, commemorating the hundredth anniversary of the firm. This original release was inscribed, thanking the workers. At the same time, the first in a series of 25 was released to the public. That series is complete and a new series began in 1997.

ARS: Latin word for "art."

ARS AG: ARS AG, Zug, Switzerland, holds the two-dimensional rights for many of the original M.I. Hummel drawings as well as the two-dimensional rights for reproductions of M.I. Hummel products made by Goebel.

Ars Edition: Ars Edition was formerly known as Ars Sacra Josef Mueller Verlag, the German publishing house that first published Hummel art, producing and selling postcards, postcard-calendars, and prints of M.I. Hummel. Today, Ars Edition GmbH is the exclusive licensee for publishing Hummel (books, calendars, cards, stationery, etc.) Owner: Marcel Nauer (grandson of Dr. Herbert Dubler).

Ars Sacra: Trademark on a gold foil label sometimes found on Hummel-like figurines produced by Herbert Dubler. This was a New York firm that produced these figurines during the years of World War II when Goebel was forbidden by the Nazi government to produce Hummel items. Ars Sacra is also the original name of the Ars Edition firm in Munich. Dubler was a son-in-law of Mr. and Mrs. Mueller, the owners of Ars Edition, formerly Ars Sacra, Munich. Although there was some corporate connection for a very short time between Mueller and Dubler, there is no connection between the Mueller Ars Sacra firm and the Hummel-like figurines produced by Dubler under the name "House of Ars Sacra" or the statement "Produced by Ars Sacra." Please see the discussion on the Dubler figures elsewhere in this volume.

Artist's Sample: See Master Sample.

Baby Bee: Describes the trademark of the factory used in 1958—a small bee flying in a V.

Backstamp: Backstamp is usually the trademark and any associated special markings on the underside of the base, the reverse, or backside of an item.

Basic Size: This term is generally synonymous with standard size. However, because the sizes listed in this book are not substantiated initial factory released sizes, it was felt that it would be misleading to label them "standard." "Basic size" was chosen to denote only an approximate standard size.

Bas-relief: A raised or sculpted design, as on the Annual Bells and the Annual Plates, as opposed to a two-dimensional painted design or decal.

Bee: A symbol used since about 1940 in various forms, as a part of or along with the factory trademark on Hummel pieces until 1979, when the bee was dropped. It was reincorporated in the special backstamp used on the M.I. Hummel exclusive pieces and a bee variation was again reinstated with new trademark (TMK-8) introduced in 2000.

Bisque: A fired but unglazed condition. Usually white but sometimes colored.

Black Germany: Term used to describe one of the various wordings found along with the Hummel trademarks on the underside of the pieces. It refers to the color used to stamp the word "Germany." Many colors have been used for the trademarks and associated marks, but black generally indicates the figure is an older mode; however, this is not an absolutely reliable indicator.

Bookends: Throughout the collection of Goebel-made Hummel items are bookends. Some are the regular figurines merely attached to wooden bookends with some type of adhesive. Some, however, are different. The latter are made without the customary base and then attached. The regular pieces, when removed from the wood, have the traditional markings. Those without the base may or may not exhibit those markings.

Candleholder: Some Hummel figurines have been produced with provisions to place candles in them.

Candy Bowl/Candy Box/Candy Dish: Small covered cylindrical box with a Hummel figurine on the top. Design changes have been made in the shape of the box/bowl/dish over the years, as well as in the manner in which the cover rests upon the bowl. See individual listings.

Closed Edition (CE): A term used by the Goebel factory to indicate that a particular item is no longer produced and will not be placed in production again.

Closed Number (CN): A term used by the Goebel factory to indicate that a particular number in the Hummel Mold Number sequence has never been used to identify an item and never will be used. A caution here: Several unquestionably genuine pieces have been found over the years bearing these so-called closed numbers.

Club Exclusive: This refers to the products made for membership premiums and sale exclusively to members of the M.I. Hummel Club. Each of these bears a special club backstamp to identify it as such.

Collector's Plaque: Same as the dealer plaque except it does not state "authorized dealer," as most later dealer plaques do. Frequently used for display with private collections (see Dealer Plaque).

Copyright Date: The actual year the original mold was made. Often the mold is made, but figures are not produced for several years afterward. The copyright date is sometimes found along with other marks on older pieces but not always. All pieces currently being produced bear a copyright date.

Crazing: A fine web-like cracked appearance in the overglaze of older porcelain and earthenware. It occurs on Hummel figurines from time to time, mostly on older pieces. See earlier section on crazing.

Crown Mark (TMK-1): One of the early W. Goebel firm trademarks. Has not been used on Hummel figurines and related pieces since sometime between 1949 and 1950.

Current Mark: For many years, this was a term describing the trademark being used at the present time. It has become a somewhat confusing term, for what is current today may not be tomorrow. Most collectors and dealers have come to use a descriptive term such as the "Crown Mark" or the use of trademark number designations such as Trademark No. 1 (TMK-1) for the Crown Mark, for instance. The number designation is usually shortened to "trademark one" when spoken or "TMK-1" when written.

Current Production: Term describing figurines, plates, candy boxes, etc. supposedly being produced at the present time. They are not necessarily readily available, because the factory maintains the molds, but doesn't always produce the figure with regularity.

Dealer Plaque: A plaque made and distributed by the Goebel firm to retailers for the purpose of advertising the fact that they are authorized dealers in Hummel figurines and related articles. The plaques always used to have the *Merry Wanderer* figure incorporated into them. Earlier models have a bumblebee perched on the top edge (see Collector's Plaque). In recent years, the figurine associated has not always been the Merry Wanderer. For more detailed information, see the listing for Hum 187.

Decimal Designator: Many earlier Goebel Hummel figurines exhibit a decimal point after the mold number, i.e.: "154." This is ostensibly to mean the same thing as the "slash" mark (/). The use of the slash mark means that there is another, smaller size of the piece either in existence, planned, or at least in prototype. There is another theory that the decimal is to make it easier to clarify the incised mold numbers and to help determine whether a number is, for instance, a 66 rather than a 99. The decimal is not always found alone with the number.

Some examples the author has observed are "49./0.", "51./0.", and "84./5."

Display Plaque: See Collector's Plaque and Dealer Plaque.

Doll Face: See Faience.

Doughnut Base: Describes a type of base used with some figures. Looking at the bottom of the base, the outer margin of the base forms a circle or oval, and a smaller circle or oval within makes the base appear doughnut-like.

Doughnut Halo: The only figures on which these appear are the Madonnas. They are formed as a solid cap type, or molded so that the figure's hair protrudes through slightly. The latter are called "Donut Halos."

Double Crown: From 1934 to 1938, there were many figures produced with two Crown WG marks. This is known as the Double Crown. One of the crowns may be a stamped crown and the other incised. Pieces have been found with both trademarks incised (see earlier section on trademarks). Thereafter, only a single Crown Mark is found.

Embossed: An erroneous term used to describe incised (see Incised).

Faience (Doll Face): Faience is defined as brilliantly glazed, bright-colored fine earthenware. More commonly called "Doll Face" pieces by collectors, this describes the few Hummel figurines that were made by Goebel in the early days of paint and finish experimentation. Several have made it into collectors' hands. Refer to the color section in the center of this book for illustrations of a few.

Fink, Emil: Publisher of a limited number of postcards and greeting cards bearing the art of M.I. Hummel. All U.S. copyrights of cards published by Fink Verlag are owned by ARS AG, Zug, Switzerland.

Font: A number of pieces have been produced with a provision for holding a small portion of holy water. They can be hung on the wall. Often referred to as Holy Water Fonts.

Full Bee (TMK-2): About 1940, the W. Goebel firm began using a bee as part of its trademark. The Full Bee trademark has been found along with the Crown trademark. The Full Bee is the first bee to be utilized. There were many versions of the Full Bee trademark. The first Full Bee is sometimes found with (R) stamped somewhere on the base.

Germany (W. GERMANY, West Germany, Western Germany): All have appeared with the trademark in several different colors.

Goebelite: This is the name the Goebel firm gives to the patented mixture of materials used to form the slip used in pouring and fashioning the earthenware Hummel figurines and other related Hummel pieces. Not often heard.

High Bee: A variation of the early Bee trademarks wherein the bee is smaller than the original bee used in the mark and flies with its wings slightly higher than the top of the V in the trademark.

Hollow Base: A base variation. Some bases for figures are solid and some are hollowed out and open into a hollow figure.

Hollow Mold: An erroneous term actually meaning Hollow Base, as above. All Hummel pieces are at least partially hollow in finished form.

Holy Water Font: See Font.

Hummel Mark (TMK-7): This mark was introduced in 1991. It is the first trademark to be used exclusively on Goebel products utilizing M.I. Hummel art for its design.

Hummel Number or Mold Number: A number or numbers incised into the base or bottom of the piece, used to identify the mold motif and sometimes the size of the figure or article. This designation is sometimes inadvertently omitted, but rarely.

Incised/Indented: Describes a mark or wording that has actually been pressed into the surface of a piece, rather than printed or stamped on the surface. It is almost always found beneath the base.

Jumbo: Sometimes used to describe the few Hummel figurines that have been produced in a substantially larger size than the normal range—usually around 30". (See Hum 7, 141, and 142.)

Light Stamp: See M.I. Hummel. It is thought that every Hummel figurine has Sister M.I. Hummel's signature stamped somewhere on it, but some apparently have no signature. In some cases, the signature may have been stamped so lightly that in subsequent painting and glazing all but unidentifiable traces are obliterated. In other cases, the signature may have been omitted altogether. The latter case is rare. The same may happen to the mold number.

Limited Edition: An item that is limited in production to a specified number or limited to the number produced in a defined period of time.

Master Sample/Mahlmuster/Master Zimmer:
This is a figurine or other item that is the model from which Goebel artists paint the newly fashioned piece. The Master Sample figurines usually have a red line painted around the flat vertical portion of the base. It is known variously in German as the Mahlmuster, Master Zimmer, Muster Zimmer, or Originalmuster. There is another notation sometimes found on the base: "Orig Arbt Muster." These are abbreviations for the German words "Original Working Model."

M.I. Hummel (Maria Innocentia Hummel):
This signature, is supposed to be applied to every Hummel article produced. However, as in Light Stamp above, it may not be evident. It is also reasonable to assume that because of the design of a particular piece or its extremely small size, it may not have been practical to place it on the piece. In such cases, a small sticker is used in its place. It is possible that these stickers became loose and were lost over the years. The signature has been found painted on in some instances but rarely. It is also possible to find the signature in decal form, brown in color. From the late-1950s to early 1960s, Goebel experimented with placing the signature on the figurines by the decal method, but abandoned the

idea. A few of the pieces the company tried it on somehow found their way into the market. Collectors should also take note of the fact that sometimes the signature appears as "Hummel" without the initials. This is also seldom found.

Mel: There are a few older Hummel figurines made by Goebel that bear this incised three-letter group along with a number. It is supposed that they were prototype pieces that were never placed in production, but at least three were.

Mold Induction Date: See Copyright Date.

Missing Bee Mark (TMK-6): In mid-1980, the Goebel company changed the trademark by removing the familiar "bee" mark collectors had grown accustomed to associating with M.I. Hummel items. It came to be known as the "Missing Bee" mark (TMK-6) for a while.

Model Number: See Mold Number.

Mold Growth: There have been many theories in the past to explain the differences in sizes of figurines marked the same and with no significant differences other than size. The explanation from Goebel is that in the earlier years of molding, the molds were made of plaster of Paris and had a tendency to wash out and erode with use. Therefore, successive use would produce pieces each being slightly larger than the last. Another possible explanation is that the firm has been known to use more than one mold simultaneously in the production of the same figure and market them with the same mold number. The company developed a synthetic resin to use instead of plaster of Paris in 1954. Although this is a vast improvement, the new material still has the same tendencies but to a significantly smaller degree.

Mold Induction Date (Copyright Date): An incorrectly used term in reference to what is actually the copyright date. See Copyright Date.

Mold Number: The official mold number used by Goebel that is unique to each Hummel item or motif used. See section on the explanation of the mold number system earlier in this chapter for an in-depth discussion.

Mother Mold Sample: When Goebel proposes a new figurine, the piece is modeled, a mother mold made, and usually three to six sample figures are produced and then painted by one of Goebel's master painters. These are for the convent and others to examine and either approve for production, suggest changes, or reject completely, as the case may be. Typically, never more than six to eight of these are produced. Sometimes the final approved models are marked with a red line and placed into service as a master sample for the artists. Although the mother mold samples do not necessarily have the red line, they are identifiable by the black ink within the incised mold number.

Mould: European spelling of Mold.

Muster Zimmer: See Master Sample.

Narrow Crown: Trademark used by the W. Goebel firm from 1937 to the early 1940s. To date, this trademark has never been found on an original Hummel piece.

One-Line Mark: See Stylized Bee.

Open Edition: Designates the Hummel figurines presently in production or in planning. It does not mean all are in production, only that it is "open" for production. Not necessarily available.

Open Number: A number in the numerical sequence of factory-designated Hummel model numbers that has not been used to identify a piece but may be used when a new design is released.

Out of Production: A confusing term sometimes used to indicate that an item is not of current production but may be placed back in production at some later date. The confusion results from the fact that some with this designation have been declared closed editions, and others have been returned to production, thus leaving all the others in the classification in limbo.

Orig Arbt Muster: A marking sometimes found beneath the base of a figurine. It is the abbreviation for the German words roughly translated to mean "Original Working Model."

Overglaze: See White Overglaze.

Oversize: A term sometimes used to describe a Hummel piece larger than that which is currently being produced. These variations could be due to mold growth (see Mold Growth).

Painter's Sample: See Master Sample.

Possible Future Edition (PFE): A term applied to Hummel mold design that does exist, but has not yet been released.

Production Mold Sample: A piece that is cast out of the first production mold.

Prototype: This is a proposed figurine or other item that must be approved by those with the authority to do so. As used by Goebel, it is further restricted to mean "the one and only sample," the first out of the mother mold. This is the one presented to the Siessen Convent for its approval/disapproval. See Mother Mold Sample.

Quartered Base: As it sounds, this is descriptive of the underside of the base of a piece being divided into four more or less equal parts.

Red Line: A red line around the outside edge of the base of a figurine means that the piece may have once served as the model for the painters.

Reinstated: A piece that is back in production after having been previously placed in a non-production status for some length of time.

Sample Model: A prototype piece modeled for the approving authorities. May or may not have gained approval. See Mother Mold Sample.

Secondary Market: When an item is bought and sold after the initial purchase, it is said to be traded on the secondary market.

Size Designator: Method of identifying the size of a figure. It is found in conjunction with the Hummel mold number on the bottom of the figure.

Slash-Marked: From time to time, a figure or a piece will be found with a slash or cut through the trademark. There are two theories as to the origin of this mark. Some think it is used to indicate a figure with some flaw or imperfection, although several figures with slash marks are, upon close examination, found to be in excellent, flawless condition. The other theory is that some figures are slash-marked to discourage resale of pieces given to or sold at a bargain price to factory workers.

Small Bee: A variation of the early Full Bee trademark wherein the bee is about half the size of the original bee.

Split Base: When viewing the bottom of the base of a piece, it appears to be split into sections. Generally refers to a base split into two sections, but could readily be used to describe more than two sections.

Stamped: A method of placing marks on the bottom of a figure wherein the data is placed on the surface rather than pressed into it (see Incised).

Standard Size: As pointed out in the section on size designators, this is a general term used to describe the size of the first figure to be produced, when there are more sizes of the same figure to be found. It is not the largest, nor the smallest, only the first. Over the years, as a result of mold design changes and possibly mold growth, all figures marked as standard are not necessarily the same size (see Basic Size).

Stylized Bee (TMK-3): About 1955, the traditional bee design in the trademark was changed to reflect a more modern "stylized" version. Also sometimes called the "One-Line Mark."

Temporarily Withdrawn: Similar to Out of Production, but in this case, it would be reasonable to assume that the piece so described will be put back into production at some future date.

Terra Cotta: Literally translated from the Latin it means "baked earth"; a naturally brownish-orange earthenware.

Three Line Mark (TMK-4): A trademark variation used in the 1960s and 1970s.

Underglaze: A term describing anything that is found underneath the glaze as opposed to being placed after the glazing.

White Overglaze: After a piece has been formed a clear glaze is applied and fired, resulting in a shiny, all-white finish.

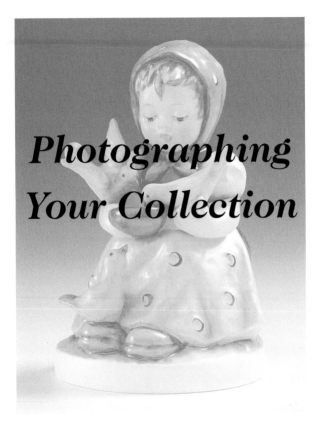

Photographing Your Collection

There are two very good reasons for taking good photographs of your collection. The most important is to have a record of what you had in the unfortunate event of a theft, fire or any other disaster that may result in the loss or destruction of your collection. Insurance companies are loathe to take your word that you had a Hum 1, *Puppy Love* worth 10 times the normal value just because its head was titled in a different direction. A photograph would prove it. In the case of theft you have little chance of identifying your collection in the event of a recovery in some instances. Law enforcement authorities often recover stolen property that can't be identified as to owner. If you have photographs of marks, etc., they can help you detailed descriptions of marks, etc., they can help you positively identify what is yours. The second reason for this section is to help you also, but it is to help me as well. I get hundreds of photos each year, most of which are useless. You

send me the photograph(s) with your questions and all I can see is what looks like a scarecrow out in the middle of a four acre field or a fuzzy Feathered Friends figurine due to its being out of focus. Can't help you much there. So, ready for your photography lesson?

This will be simple and fun for most of you. It won't make you America's next Ansel Adams, but it will make you a better photographer of figurines. You experts and pros can move on to the next section now.

The Camera

The two most common cameras most of us use today are the 35mm single lens reflex (SLR) and the automatic "point and shoot" cameras that use the mini negative disc or regular 35mm film. The method for taking the kind of photographs we are looking for here differs between the types so we will go through the basic set-up to get your figurines ready to shoot and then describe the method for each of the camera types.

Setting

I employ a light blue or gray paper background normally that starts flat on a table top and is rolled up behind the figurine forming a curved background so there is no horizontal line to distract from the figure. You probably won't want to get that elaborate so go out and get a sheet of poster board. I recommend a light gray, pale blue or beige for a neutral background. First try to set it up as I described before, rolling it up. If you are not successful that way, try cutting it in half, putting one piece flat on the table top and the other propped up somehow behind it as in the diagram. The diagram is overly simple and out of scale, but illustrates the idea.

If this set-up is more than you want to try, a simple tabletop or any flat surface will suffice. Try to avoid any with a patterned surface.

Lighting

There are two types of light: natural (or available) light and artificial light.

Natural Light

The simplest and best light is natural light outdoors, on an overcast day or in the shade on a bright sunshiny day. This eliminates harsh shadows. You can get almost the same light indoors if you shoot your picture at a large window that is admitting much light but not letting direct sunlight in.

Artificial Light

If you wish to shoot inside under artificial light

you can do so in a bright, well-lighted room. You must be careful, however, about the type of light you have. Fluorescent lighting will produce pictures with a decidedly greenish cast. Incandescent lighting, ordinary light bulbs, will cause your pictures to come out with a yellowish or red cast. This is true when using ordinary, daylight color film designed for use outdoors or with a flash. Most modern photo processing labs can filter this color distortion out, but you must tell them about the type of light you used beforehand.

Using a flash is the third possibility, but under ordinary circumstances produces a severe, flat picture with harsh shadows.

If you can devise a way of filtering the flash, diffusing it or bouncing it off the ceiling or any other reflector you can devise, results are generally much more satisfying. The best use of flash is for "fill light" when shooting outdoors. It fills in shadows, eliminating them if done right.

Choice of Film

Film comes in different speeds (ASA ratings). The higher the ASA the faster the speed. The faster the speed, the less light needed to take a good photograph. There is a trade-off, however. The faster the speed the grainier the picture. This should not be of concern to you unless you are going to enlarge the picture or submit it for publications. I recommend that you use film with an ASA of 100 or 200, but if you have a poor light situation the ASA 400 would give you satisfactory pictures. Those of you with the modern automatic cameras shouldn't need to worry about switching these ASA's because your camera will automatically adjust to the ASA. Be sure to read your manual about this (You did read your manual didn't you?). Those of you with the more complicated SLR's know what to do.

General Techniques

First, you have a choice of methods. If you are shooting the pictures for instance purposes you may choose to make a gang shot; that is shooting of two or three or more at the same time, or shooting your display cabinets or shelves (if there is a glass door, be sure to open it first). The latter is less desirable because you lose the detail you may need for identification later. If you don't wish to shoot each individual piece, then shoot them in groups of no more than three or four and try to match sizes as best you can.

When you take your pictures get in as close as you can, filling the frame with the figures. Try to hold the camera as low and level with the pieces as you can unless this causes a hand or some other part of the figure to obscure or cast a shadow on a face or other important features. Sometimes adjusting the position of the figure can alleviate this problem. Remember, you want to show it at its best. If your camera is capable of close-up photography or there is a close-up lens attachment for it, take shots of the underside of the base of each piece or at least of the most valuable ones. These close-up attachments are usually quite inexpensive and come in sets of three lens.

Technique for Automatic Cameras

Most of the automatic cameras of today come with a fixed focus lens or an automatic focus feature. Some even have a "macro" feature allowing you to get a little closer than normal to your subject. This feature allows somewhat nicer close-up portraiture, but is not of much use for our purposes here. Most automatic cameras will not allow you to get any closer than three feet from your subject. Any closer and everything will be out of focus. The field of view at three feet will be about 20" x 24". If you put one 6" figurine in the middle of that, take the picture and process it, you will get a photo about 4" x 5" in size and the figurine will be less than 1-1/4" tall, a lonesome trifling tidbit in the center. (Remember the scarecrow in the 40-acre field?) It would be of little use in identification. A few of these cameras have close-up attachments available so check your manual to see if yours is one of them. If not then you will at best, only be able to make group pictures. You might want to experiment with one roll of film. Some of the automatic cameras will do much more than others and some will do better than the manual indicates. If your experiment is a failure, I suggest you prevail upon a friend or relative who has a better camera to help you out. Better yet, go out and buy one. The single lens reflex cameras are not nearly as complicated to use as they appear, and some of the new, electronic ones make it almost impossible to take a bad picture.

Technique for Single Lens Reflex Camera

Chances are many of you who have SLRs have never tried to do macro work. That is what small object photography is called. If you have perfected that art, you have permission to skip the rest of this section.

Macrophotography is a big word for a relatively simple technique, the results of which can be quite rewarding. In fact many of the photos in this book were shot with a Honeywell Pentax SLR with a standard 55mm lens that I bought many years ago. Many of you will probably have much newer and better cameras than mine. Your camera should do as well as the one I have. Mine will focus down to about 13" from the subject with a 5" x 7" field of view and with a set of inexpensive close-up lens (less than $25), you can get spectacular close-ups. Remember though, the more magnification you get, the less depth of field is available. I may have lost some of you there. Depth of field is simply the area in front of the camera that will photograph with acceptable sharpness. Said another way, it is the difference between the nearest and the furthest point of acceptable sharpness or focus in the scene to be photographed.

Focusing and Depth of Field

The depth of field you will be connected with here is a function of the F-stop for the photograph and to a lesser extent, the distance from the lens to the subject. Simply put, the higher the F-stop selected, the more depth of field you have. It varies with the lens but the depth of field on my camera at F-16 is about 3" when it is focused as close as possible. When I focus on a figurine I try to focus about midway into its depth. This is entirely sufficient to keeping all parts of the figurine in focus in most cases. You may be able to do a little better or a little worse depending on your lens. Although you will likely be working as close to the subject as you can get, you should know that the further you get from the subject, the more the depth of field.

Shutter Speeds and F-stops

We have already noted that you will want to use a high F-stop number, F-11 or higher. Well the higher the F-stop, the smaller the aperture (the hole through which the reflected light passes on its way to the film). The smaller that hole is the longer it takes enough light reflected from your subject to form a good image on the film. So it follows that the smaller the hole the longer the shutter must remain open. Since we want enough depth of field so that all of a figurine is in focus, we'll have to trade off for time. That means the shutter speed will be too slow for you to hand-hold your camera. That is why you will need to buy or borrow a tripod. Some folks are clever enough to jury-rig one. It would also be a good idea to have a cable release to insure that you do not shake the camera when tripping the shutter. They are inexpensive and available anywhere good cameras are sold.

Shooting the Picture

Here is a typical set-up in sufficient light to take your pictures:

Film speed	ASA 100 to 200
Shutter speed	1/8 to 1/30
F-stop	F-11 to F-16
Focal distance	14" to 18"; as close as you can or need to be.

You will likely need to experiment a little until you are happy with the results. There are 12 print rolls of film available if you don't wish to waste film. The best way to find the ideal set-up for your light conditions is to shoot at different F-stops, leaving everything else constant, and place a piece of paper with your subject with the setting written on it or do the same thing varying any setting you want. You then will have a set of photos from which to pick the best and have the best camera setting right there in the picture.

Some Final Notes

This listing is taken from the Suggested Retail Price List issued by Goebel in 2002. It is the published suggested retail price for the figures and other items that bear the trademark presently being used by the company (TMK-8). The appearance of a particular piece on this list is not necessarily an indication that it is available from dealers. Few dealers have the wherewithal to pick their stock and even fewer have the ability to have a large, comprehensive stock.

The abbreviation "TW" in the place of a retail price means that the item has been "Temporarily Withdrawn" from current production with no stated date for reinstatement. Other pieces may be absent from the list. Those have been removed from production or retired.

References and Organizations

Recommended Books for Collectors

Aaseng, Nathan. *The Unsung Heroes: Unheralded People Who Invented Famous Products.* Lerner Publications Co., Minneapolis, MN 55401. Eight people are included in this book for young readers. Among them are the inventors of Coca-Cola, McDonald's hamburgers, and vacuum cleaners. "Sister Maria Innocentia's Gift, M.I. Hummel Figurines" is the relevant chapter.

Arbenz, Pat. *Hummel Facts.* Misty's Gift Gallery, 228 Fry Blvd., Sierra Vista, AZ 85635. A reprint collection of all Mr. Arbenz' columns for *Plate Collector* magazine. Indispensable to the collector. Although inexpensive, it is out of print and difficult to find. You might try contacting Arbenz: he may have a few copies.

Armke, Ken. *Hummel: An Illustrated Handbook and Price Guide.* Published by Wallace-Homestead, c/o Krause Publications, 700 E. State St., Iola, WI 54990. 1995. This full-color guide is of much practical use to the collector. Well researched, well written, and interesting.

ArsEdition. *The Hummel.* Verlag Ars Sacra Josef Mueller, Munich, Germany, 1984. A 78-page, full-color hardcover book, full of illustrations by Sister M.I. Hummel and light verse.

Authentic *Hummel Figurines*. Copyright by W. Goebel, Rodental, Germany. An illustrated catalog that was for many years published by the company. Out of print.

Ehrmann, Erich and Robert L. Miller (special contributor). *Hummel, The Complete Collector's Guide and Illustrated Reference*. Portfolio Press Corporation, Huntington, NY 11743. 1976. Ehrmann, publisher of Collectors Editions magazine, and Miller, acknowledged expert and owner of one of the world's largest Hummel collections, collaborated to present this large work. As a reference it is invaluable to collectors.

Ehrmann, Erich W., Robert L. Miller and Walter Pfeiffer. *M.I. Hummel: The Golden Anniversary Album*. Portfolio Press Corporation, Huntington, NY 11743. 1984. A beautiful book full of color photos and much good information for collectors.

Guide for Collectors. Copyright by W. Goebel, Rodental, Germany. Available through the M.I. Hummel Club, P.O. Box 11, Pennington, NJ 08534-0011. A beautiful, large-format, full-color catalog of the current Goebel M.I. Hummel collection including closed editions. It is updated periodically.

Hotchkiss, John. *Hummel Art*. 3rd edition. Wallace-Homestead Book Co., c/o Krause Publications, 700 E. State St., Iola, WI 54990. 1982. A full-color handbook that essentially updates the first and second editions. Out of print.

Hummel, Berta and Margarete Seeman. *The Hummel Book*. 17th edition. W. Goebel, Rodental, Germany, 1992. This copyright is today with ARS AG, Zug, Switzerland.

Hummel, Maria Innocentia. Hummel: *The Original Illustrations of Sister Maria Innocentia Hummel*. Courage Books. 1998. 144 pages.

Hunt, Dick. *Goebel Miniatures of Robert Olzewski*. 595 Jackson Ave., Satellite Beach, FL. Hunt's Collectibles.

Koller, Angelica. *The Hummel*. Released by ArsEdition in 1995, this book describes Berta Hummel's childhood and her life as a nun. It also explains her theory of art and includes many full-color reproductions of her art. Hardcover, 141 pages. Available through your dealer or the M.I. Hummel Club.

Luckey, Carl F. (edited by Dean A. Genth). *Luckey's Hummel Figurines and Plates*. 12th edition. Krause Publications, 700 E. State St., Iola, WI 54990. 2002. The most comprehensive collector's reference on the market today. Not only does it cover all of the W. Goebel Porzellanfabrik three-dimensional M.I. Hummel figurines and related items, but also all of the hundreds of other available Hummel collectibles. Chock full of great pictures and useful and fascinating information. 550 pages. Available at most booksellers.

M.I. Hummel Album. Portfolio Press Corporation, Huntington, NY 11743. 1992. A beautiful full-color reference showing most of the figurines ever made. Of particular interest is the illustration of many possible future editions (PFE). A Goebel publication. See your dealer or contact the M.I. Hummel Club.

Miller, Robert L. *Hummel.* Portfolio Press Corporation, Huntington, NY 11743. 1979. This is a supplement to the original Hummel, the *Complete Collector's Guide and Illustrated Reference* by Ehrmann and Miller.

Miller, Robert L. *M.I. Hummel Figurines, Plates, More ...* 8th edition. Portfolio Press Corporation, Huntington, NY 11743. 2000. A well-organized and handy reference by this noted collector.

Miller, Robert L. *Hummels 1978-1998: 20 Years of "Miller on Hummel" Columns.* From Collector's News. 1998. 246 pages.

Plaut, James S. Formation of an Artist, *The Early Works of Berta Hummel*. Schmid Brothers, Inc., Randolph, MA, 1980. This softbound book is actually a catalog of the 1980-82 tour of an exhibition of paintings, drawings, photographs, and a tapestry from the collection of the Hummel family.

Saal, Kathleen *In the Land of Hummel: Traditional Bavarian Life*. Portfolio Press Corporation, Huntington, NY 11743. 1999. 160 pages. Photographer Walter Pfeiffer.

Schwatlo, Wolfgang. *M.I. Hummel Collector's Handbook*. Schwatlo GMBH, D65522 Niedernhausen, Postfach 1224, Germany, 1994. This full-color handbook is of great value to the collector. It concentrates on the many variations that can be found and includes color photographs. A must for the serious collector.

Schwatlo, Wolfgang. *M.I. Hummel Collector's Handbook with Prices*. Schwatlo GmbH, D-65522 Niedernhausen, Postfach 1224, Germany, 1996. An update of Schwatlo's 1994 book. This edition has been expanded to include many other related collectibles. It is full-color and bilingual. A very useful book for the serious collector.

Struss, Dieter. *M.I. Hummel Figuren*. Weltbild Verlag GmbH, Augsburg, Bavaria, Germany, 1993. A full-color hardbound collector's guide (in German).

Wiegand, Sister M. Gonsalva, O.S.F. *Sketch Me Berta Hummel*. Reprinted by Robert L. Miller and available at most dealers or from Miller at P.O. Box 210, Eaton, OH 45320.

Wonsch, Lawrence L. *Hummel Copycats*. Wallace-Homestead, c/o Krause Publications, 700 E. State St., Iola, WI 54990. 1987. A superb treatment of the hundreds of copies of M.I. Hummel figurines over the years and around the world.

Videotapes

A Hummel Christmas. Cascom International, Inc., 806 4th Ave. So., Nashville, TN 37210. 1995. An enchanting production about 30 minutes long, this video boasts a masterful blend of rare figurines, original M.I. Hummel art, special effects, and Christmas music. This is a must-have video for the Christmas season for any lover of Hummel figurines and art.

M.I. Hummel Marks of Distinction. A historical look at the progression of M.I. Hummel backstamps from the beginning to the current mark. Available from the M.I. Hummel Club.

The Insider's Guide to M.I. Hummel Collecting.
Bottom Line Productions, Inc., 1994. This
one-hour video features M.I. Hummel Club
spokesperson Gwen Toma in an excellent
presentation of the various marks and
backstamps found on the figurines and related
items. An excellent overview of how they are
produced, as well as an explanation of how the
figurines are painted by Goebel Master Artist
Sigrid Then. The greatest part of the video is
given over to a charming sequence by Bob and
Ruth Miller, who give you a personal tour of
some of the more rare and interesting pieces in
their famous collection. Available from the M.I.
Hummel Club.

The Life of Sister M.I. Hummel. Produced by W.
Goebel. This is a striking 25-minute treatment
of Berta Hummel's life. Available from the M.I.
Hummel Club.

Periodicals

The following is a list of periodicals you may find
useful in collecting Hummel figurines.

> *Antiques Journal* (monthly)
> P.O. Box 1046
> Dubuque, IA 52001

Has occasional articles about Hummel collecting and ads for buying and selling Hummels.

The Antique Trader Weekly (weekly)
700 E. State St.
Iola, WI 54990
Occasional Hummel articles and extensive ads for buying and selling Hummel items.

Collector Editions (quarterly)
170 Fifth Avenue
New York, NY 10010
Has occasional Hummel column.

Collectors Journal (weekly)
Box 601
Vinton, IA 52349
Has ads for Hummel buying and selling.

Collectors Mart (bimonthly)
700 E. State St.
Iola, WI 54990

Collectors News (monthly)
606 8th Street
Grundy Center, IA 50638
Has ads for Hummel buying and selling and occasional Hummel articles.

Collectors' Showcase (bimonthly)
P.O. Box 6929
San Diego, CA 92106

The Tri-State Trader (weekly)
P.O. Box 90
Knightstown, IN 46148
Has ads for Hummel buying and selling.

Clubs and Organizations

There are a few dealers and manufacturers who sponsor "collector's clubs." They are designed to market their products to a target audience. This is a good marketing technique that doubles as a means of educating collectors as to what artists and manufacturers are presently doing. The collector of M.I. Hummel items is lucky to have a couple of these. They are unique in that they are very large organizations and are very serious about keeping collectors informed. Both organizations offer a very valuable member figurine sales and wanted list. Membership in both is highly recommended.

The Hummel Collector's Club, Inc.

1261 University Drive
P.O. Box 157
Yardley, PA 19067
(888) 5-HUMMEL (toll-free)

This club was established in 1975 by Dorothy Dous. She and her husband developed the club into a very valuable organization for collectors of Hummel collectibles. Mrs. Dous (Dottie) writes an interesting quarterly newsletter that is lengthy, easy to read, and crammed with information. The newsletter also includes a long list of members' for-sale, trade, or wanted lists. The club acts as a gratis go-between for its members. Any collector would benefit by becoming a member of this organization.

The M.I. Hummel Club

Goebel Plaza
P.O. Box 11
Pennington, NJ 08534-0011
(609) 737-8777, (800) 666-2582 (toll-free)
www.mihummel.com

This club was founded by the W. Goebel firm in 1976 as the Goebel Collectors' Club and became the M.I. Hummel Club in the spring of 1989. The club publishes a beautiful and very informative full-color quarterly newsletter, *Insights*, which no collector should be without. Another advantage of membership is the renewal gifts each year, usually a figurine, and the chance to buy figures that are offered exclusively to members and are specially marked with the club backstamp. They also maintain a referral list of members' items for sale or wanted. In 2002, the M.I. Hummel Club celebrated its 25th anniversary. Check the Web site for current exclusive offerings and events.

Local Chapters of the M.I. Hummel Club

At least 143 local chapters of the M.I. Hummel Club were active in 41 states and 4 provinces in Canada as of October 1996. There is even an International Chapter for members with the name "Hummel" as their surname or maiden name. If you are interested in joining a local chapter or starting one of your own, call or write the club in Pennington, New Jersey (information listed earlier in this chapter).

United States

Arizona

Roadrunner (Phoenix)

Yuma

Arkansas

Arkansas Traveler (Magnolia)

California

Camarillo

Central Coast (Lompoc)

Fresno
Heart of the Redwoods (Eureka)
Orange County
Pleasant Valley (Camarillo)
San Bernardino (Yucaipa)
San Diego County
San Francisco East Bay
San Gabriel (Covina)
Silicon Valley (San Jose)
Whittier (West Hills)

Colorado

Gateway to the Rockies (Aurora)
Loveland Sweetheart (Fort Collins)
Mile Hi (Denver)
Pikes Peak (Colorado Springs)

Connecticut

Central (Plantsville)
Rose City (Norwich)

Florida

Daytona Beach
Delray Beach
Fivay
Ft. Lauderdale (Closed)
Greater Zephryhills
Jacksonville
Leesburg

Ocala
Orlando Area
Palm Beach
Seven Rivers (Beverly Hills)
Suncoast (Palm Harbor)
Tampa Area (Closed)
The Villages of Lady Lake

Georgia

Augusta (Evans)
Metro Atlanta (Dallas)

Illinois

Batavia Travelers
Gateway East (Belleville)
Greater Peoria Area
Illiana (Valpariso)
LaGrange Park (Bridgeview)
McHenry County
Northern Illinois (Crystal Lake)
N.W. Suburban (Palatine)

Indiana

Danville (Avon)
Hoosier Connection (Russiaville)

Kansas

Mo-Kan (Kansas City)
North Central Kansas (Salina)
Sunflower (McPherson)

Louisiana
Cajun Collectors (Baton Rouge)

Maine
Nor'Easter (Auburn)

Maryland
Eventide (Easton)
Pleasant Journey (Crownsville)
Silver Spring

Massachusetts
Cape Cod (Sandwich)
Neponset Valley (Dedham)
Pioneer Valley (West Springfield)
Quabbin (Ludlow)

Michigan
Adventurous Anglers (Tipton) (Closed)
Dearborn
Great Lakes (Dearborn)
Niles Saginaw Valley (Bay City)

Missouri
St. Louis Spirit of the River (Ballwin)

Montana
Big Sky (Great Falls)
Yellowstone (Billings)

Nebraska
Cinderella (Lincoln)

Huskers (Lincoln)
Omaha

Nevada
High Sierra

New Hampshire
Graniteer (Manchester)

New Jersey
Friendly Hands (NJ and NY)
Jersey Cape (Absecon)
Ocean Pines (Forked River)

New Mexico
Albuquerque

New York
Great South Bay (Massapequa)
Nassau-Suffolk (New Hyde Park)
Northern Catskills (Hunter)
Paumanok (Closed)
Rochester (Hilton)
Tonawanda Valley (Attica)
Western NY (Getzville)

North Carolina
Carolina Mountain Region (Flat Rock)
Hornet's Nest (Concord)

Ohio
Firelands Area (Sandusky)

Greater Cleveland
Miami Valley (Beavercreek)
Stark County Hall of Fame (N. Canton)
Toledo (Archbold)
Queen City (Cincinnati)
Youngstown/Hubbard

Oklahoma

OK Chapter (Oklahoma City)

Oregon

Cascade (Eugene)
Portland (Tigard)

Pennsylvania

Antietam Valley (Waynesboro)
Berks County (Kutztown)
Bux-Mont (Bucks & Montgomery Counties)
Central (Miffinburg)
Schuylkill County (Hamburg)
York County (Spring Grove)

South Carolina

Piedmont Carolinas (Charlotte)

Tennessee

Knoxville (Friendsville)

Texas

Alamo (San Antonio)
Brazosport (Lake Jackson)

Dallas Metroplex (Frisco)
Fort Worth
Gulf Coast (Houston)
Hill County Hummels

Utah

Beehive
Cache Bridgerland

Vermont

Burlington (Essex Junction)

Virginia

Gentle Care (West Springfield) (Closed)
Northern Virginia (Springfield)
Tidewater Area (Chesapeake)
West Richmond (Glen Allen)

Washington

Bellevue (Closed)
Puget Sound (Marysville)
Seattle-Tacoma (Edmonds)

West Virginia

Almost Heaven (Morgantown)

Wisconsin

Fox Valley (Fond du Lac)
Mad City West (Middleton)
Milwaukee

Canada

Alberta
Calgary
Calgary (Alberta)
Edmonton (Sherwood Park)

British Columbia
Greater Vancouver (Langley)

Saskatchewan
Saskatoon

International

Club members with "Hummel" as their surnames or maiden names. There is also a group of International M.I. Hummel Clubs in Europe.

Hummel figurines are quite inspiring on many levels. They evoke responses in those who collect them ranging from joy to quiet reflection. Remember to collect the pieces that attract you, and take time to enjoy these treasures that touch your heart.

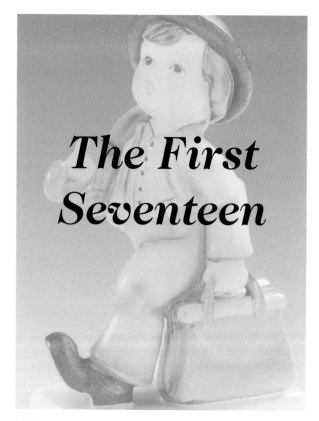

The First Seventeen

Hum No. 1 *Puppy Love,* **$305-$1000**

For purposes of simplification the various trademarks have been abbreviated in the list. Should you encounter any trouble interpreting the abbreviations, refer to the list below.

Trademark	*Abbreviations*	*Dates*
Crown	TMK-1	1934-1950
Full Bee	TMK-2	1940-1959
Stylized Bee	TMK-3	1958-1972
Three Line Mark	TMK-4	1964-1972
Last Bee	TMK-5	1972-1979
Missing Bee	TMK-6	1979-1991
Hummel Mark	TMK-7	1991-1999
Millennium Bee (Current)	TMK-8	2000-present

Hum 1: Puppy Love

Part of the original 46 pieces offered in 1935, *Puppy Love* was first known as the "*Little Violinist.*" It was first modeled by master sculptor Arthur Moeller in 1935 and can be found in Crown Mark (TMK-1) through TMK-6. It was retired in 1988, never to be produced again.

Many of the original group of 46 have been found rendered in terra cotta, and *Puppy Love* is no exception, although so far, only one is known to exist in any private collection. It has an incised Crown Mark and incised number "T-1." It is valued at $4000-$5000.

The most significant variation occurs in Crown pieces only. In this variation, the head is tilted slightly to the right instead of the typical left, he wears a black hat, and there is no necktie. This very rare variation can bring $4000-$5000 on the collector market.

It is possible, though unlikely, that you may encounter a mold number variation of this piece. It seems that in the initial stages of planning and modeling the figurines, there was no formal designation of the mold number, and *Puppy Love* has been found with the mold number FF 15. If found, this early sample with the original number is worth $5000-$10,000.

A third early sample was produced in 1935 by Arthur Moeller and is similar to *Little Hiker* (Hum 16/I) with an attached pot. If found, this piece would be worth $5000-$10,000.

Hum No.	Basic Size	Trademark	Current Value
1	5"	TMK-1	$755-$1000
1	5"	TMK-2	$550-$600
1	5"	TMK-3	$510-$550
1	5"	TMK-4	$400-$510
1	5"	TMK-5	$350-$400
1	5"	TMK-6	$305-$350

Hum 2: Little Fiddler

Originally known as the "*Violinist*" and then "*The Wandering Fiddler*," this little fellow is almost always wearing a brown derby with an orange hatband. Modeled by master sculptor Arthur Moeller in 1935, the figure has been made in five sizes since its initial introduction as part of the original 46.

The two largest sizes were temporarily withdrawn from production in 1989. The smallest, Hum 2/4/0, was introduced into the line in 1984 and was temporarily withdrawn from the North American market on December 31, 1997.

A few *Little Fiddlers* with the Crown Mark (TMK-1) have been found in doll face or faience finish. These are valued at about 20% more than the regular Crown pieces, or $5000-$6000.

A mold number variation has been found with the mold number FF 16. In the days before the figurines were given the official "Hum" designation, the "FF" was used (on the first three models). It is possible, but not likely, that you will encounter this variation. If found, it would be worth $5000-$10,000.

Goebel produced a limited edition of 50 Hum 2/I pieces in 1985 for a company-sponsored contest in Europe to celebrate 50 years of M.I. Hummel figurines. The limited edition had a gold painted

Hum No. 2 *Little Fiddler*, $130-$4000

base and special backstamp that read, "50 Jahre M.I. Hummel-Figuren 1935-1985." These are worth $1500-$2000.

Recently, a 12-1/4" version of *Little Fiddler* was introduced as part of the "Millennium Love" series, which also included *Sweet Music* (Hum 186/III), *Serenade* (Hum 85/III), *Band Leader* (Hum 129/III), and *Soloist* (Hum 135/III). These oversized pieces (Hum 85/III) were in limited supply and had to be special-ordered through an authorized M.I. Hummel retailer.

Hum No.	Basic Size	Trademark	Current Value
2/4/0	3-1/2"	TMK-6	$130-$140
2/0	6"	TMK-1	$700-$850
2/0	6"	TMK-2	$430-$500
2/0	6"	TMK-3	$350-$400
2/0	6"	TMK-4	$325-$350
2/0	6"	TMK-5	$275-$300
2/0	6"	TMK-6	$260-$275
2/0	6"	TMK-7	$260-$275
2/0	6"	TMK-8	$260
2/I	7-1/2"	TMK-1	$1110-$1500
2/I	7-1/2"	TMK-2	$650-$930
2/I	7-1/2"	TMK-3	$565-$650

Hum No.	Basic Size	Trademark	Current Value
2/I	7-1/2"	TMK-4	$460-$560
2/I	7-1/2"	TMK-5	$425-$435
2/I	7-1/2"	TMK-6	$415-$420
2/II	11"	TMK-1	$2500-$3500
2/II	11"	TMK-2	$1800-$2300
2/II	11"	TMK-3	$1515-$1600
2/II	11"	TMK-4	$1300-$1515
2/II	11"	TMK-5	$1200-$1300
2/II	11"	TMK-6	$1110-$1200
2/III	12-1/4"	TMK-1	$3500-$4000
2/III	12-1/4"	TMK-2	$2310-$2800
2/III	12-1/4"	TMK-3	$1600-$1800
2/III	12-1/4"	TMK-4	$1400-$1600
2/III	12-1/4"	TMK-5	$1300-$1400
2/III	12-1/4"	TMK-6	$1205-$1300
2/III	12-1/4"	TMK-8	$1550

Hum 3: Book Worm

One of the original 46 released in 1935, the piece was modeled by master sculptor Arthur Moeller in 1935. This figure (a girl reading a book) appears more than once in the collection and was originally called *"Little Book Worm."* It is also found in a smaller size as Hum 8 and in the Hum 14/A and 14/B bookends with a companion figure of a boy reading (*Book Worms*).

The larger Hum 3/II and Hum 3/III have been out of current production for some time.

The Hum 3/III with older trademarks is avidly sought by collectors.

The numbers 3/II and 3/III are occasionally found with the Arabic number size designator (3/2 and 3/3 respectively).

The two larger sizes (8" and 9-1/2") have been temporarily withdrawn from current production.

There is a mold number variation. Before the figurines were given "Hum" mold numbers this figure was given the incised mold number FF 17. It is possible, but not likely, that you will encounter this variation. If found, it is worth $5000-$10,000.

Additionally, a few faience pieces have surfaced. These are valued at $3000-$5000.

Hum No. 3 *Book Worm,* $365-$4000

Hum No.	Basic Size	Trademark	Current Value
3/I	5-1/2"	TMK-1	$900-$1110
3/I	5-1/2"	TMK-2	$600-$700
3/I	5-1/2"	TMK-3	$475-$500
3/I	5-1/2"	TMK-4	$400-$475
3/I	5-1/2"	TMK-5	$380-$400
3/I	5-1/2"	TMK-6	$370-$380
3/I	5-1/2"	TMK-7	$365-$370
3/I	5-1/2"	TMK-8	$370
3/II	8"	TMK-1	$2500-$3500
3/II	8"	TMK-2	$1800-$2300
3/II	8"	TMK-3	$1500-$1600
3/II	8"	TMK-4	$1300-$1500
3/II	8"	TMK-5	$1200-$1300
3/II	8"	TMK-6	$1110-$1200
3/III	9-1/2"	TMK-1	$3500-$4000
3/III	9-1/2"	TMK-2	$2300-$2800
3/III	9-1/2"	TMK-3	$1600-$1800
3/III	9-1/2"	TMK-4	$1460-$1600
3/III	9-1/2"	TMK-5	$1360-$1460
3/III	9-1/2"	TMK-6	$1250-$1360

Hum 4: Little Fiddler

This is the same design as the Hum 2, *Little Fiddler*. The difference is, of course, that this is a smaller size than any of the original three sizes of the Hum 2. It too was modeled by master sculptor Arthur Moeller in 1935. One wonders why the company used two different mold numbers for the same basic piece in the original 46 released in 1935.

Another difference is that this variation (Hum 4) wears a black hat.

There is a significant variation found in some of the Crown Mark (TMK-1) pieces. The head is tilted to his right instead of the usual tilt to his left and he wears no tie. This variation can fetch up $3000-$4000 on the collector market. Refer to the color section to see a photo of a Hum 4 with this variation that is also in the faience finish.

The mold number is sometimes found with the decimal point (4.) designator, which can increase its value by up to 10%.

Hum No.	Basic Size	Trademark	Current Value
4	4-3/4"	TMK-1	$650-$800
4	4-3/4"	TMK-2	$400-$500
4	4-3/4"	TMK-3	$325-$375
4	4-3/4"	TMK-4	$300-$325

Hum No. 4 *Little Fiddler,* $240-$800

Hum No.	Basic Size	Trademark	Current Value
4	4-3/4"	TMK-5	$270-$300
4	4-3/4"	TMK-6	$250-$270
4	4-3/4"	TMK-7	$245-$250
4	4-3/4"	TMK-8	$240

Hum 5: Strolling Along

One of the first 46 figures released in 1935, Hum 5 appears in only one basic size, 4-3/4". This figure, which is similar to *Merry Wanderer* (Hum 7), was modeled by Arthur Moeller in 1935.

The most notable variation found in Hum 5 is that TMK-6 figures have the boy looking straight ahead, while the older ones have him looking to the side. There is also evidence that a sample was produced with an attached pot, similar to *Little Hiker* (Hum 16/I) and if found, that piece is worth $5,000-$10,000.

Strolling Along was removed from production at the end of 1989, never to be made again.

Hum No.	Basic Size	Trademark	Current Value
5	4-3/4"	TMK-1	$700-$950
5	4-3/4"	TMK-2	$500-$600

Hum No. 5 *Strolling Along,* $275-$950

Hum No.	Basic Size	Trademark	Current Value
5	4-3/4"	TMK-3	$450-$500
5	4-3/4"	TMK-4	$350-$450
5	4-3/4"	TMK-5	$300-$350
5	4-3/4"	TMK-6	$275-$300

Hum 6: Sensitive Hunter

Called *The Timid Hunter* when first released among the original 46, this figure has remained in production ever since. Like the other originals, it was modeled by Arthur Moeller in 1935.

The most notable variation is the "H" shape of the suspenders used with the lederhosen. This variation is associated with all of the Crown Mark (TMK-1) figures and most of those with the Full Bee (TMK-2). The "H" variation will generally bring about 30% more than the value for the "X" pieces.

The later models have an "X" shape configuration. Crown Mark pieces have been found having the "X" shape suspenders. The color of the rabbit was usually orange, until 1981 when the company changed it to brown for all newly produced pieces.

Sensitive Hunter can also be found with the decimal (6.) designator. This can add up to 10% to its collector value.

The smallest of the sizes listed here, Hum 6/2/0, was added in 1985 as the second in a series of new smaller figurines matching mini-plates of the same design.

On December 31, 1984, Goebel announced the 7-1/2" size (Hum 6/II) was temporarily withdrawn from production status. In January 1999, the smallest size (6 2/0) was temporarily withdrawn. And as of June 15, 2002, the 4-3/4" size (6/0) also was temporarily withdrawn.

Hum No.	Basic Size	Trademark	Current Value
6/2/0	4"	TMK-6	$175-$180
6/2/0	4"	TMK-7	$170-$175
6	4-3/4"	TMK-1	$850-$1000
6/0	4-3/4"	TMK-1	$650-$800
6/0	4-3/4"	TMK-2	$400-$500
6/0	4-3/4"	TMK-3	$325-$350
6/0	4-3/4"	TMK-4	$300-$325
6/0	4-3/4"	TMK-5	$275-$300
6/0	4-3/4"	TMK-6	$250-$275
6/0	4-3/4"	TMK-7	$245-$250
6/0	4-3/4"	TMK-8	$240
6/I	5-1/2"	TMK-1	$850-$1000
6/I	5-1/2"	TMK-2	$500-$600

Hum No. 6 *Sensitive Hunter*, $170-$2000

Hum No.	Basic Size	Trademark	Current Value
6/I	5-1/2"	TMK-3	$375-$425
6/I	5-1/2"	TMK-4	$350-$375
6/I	5-1/2"	TMK-5	$325-$350
6/I	5-1/2"	TMK-6	$300-$325
6/II	7-1/2"	TMK-1	$1500-$2000
6/II	7-1/2"	TMK-2	$955-$1255
6/II	7-1/2"	TMK-3	$550-$650
6/II	7-1/2"	TMK-4	$475-$550
6/II	7-1/2"	TMK-5	$425-$475
6/II	7-1/2"	TMK-6	$350-$425

Hum 7: Merry Wanderer

One of the original 46 figurines released in 1935, the same design also appears as Hum 11. Originally modeled by master sculptor Arthur Moeller, the *Merry Wanderer* is probably found in more sizes and variations than any other single figure in the collection. There are at least 12 different sizes known to exist. There is even a huge 6-foot concrete replica of the figure on the factory grounds in Germany. An 8-foot-high *Merry Wanderer* was displayed on the grounds of the former location of the M.I. Hummel Club in Tarrytown, New York, and subsequently was placed in storage for several years. It is now displayed at the Donald E. Stephens Museum of Hummels in Rosemont, Illinois.

It is also part of every dealer and collector's display plaque made prior to the 1986 introduction of the Tally display plaque, Hum 460. In 1990, the *Merry Wanderer* display plaque was reintroduced.

The rarest of sizes is the Hum 7/III, which was temporarily withdrawn from production in 1991.

The rarest of the base variations is illustrated in the accompanying photograph. Collectors refer to it variously as the "double step base," "stepped-up base," or the "stair step base." It is found on the Hum 7/I size of all the Crown Mark (TMK-1) and Full Bee (TMK-2) 7/I pieces, but only on the older Stylized Bee (TMK-3) pieces.

The 7/III size has been found in the faience finish. These can bring up to 20% to 50% more than the top value for the Crown Mark pieces.

The 2002 Goebel Suggested Retail Price List places a $26,550 value on the 32" "Jumbo" *Merry Wanderer*. The few "Jumbo" figures in private collectors' hands are generally used as promotional figures in showrooms and shops. They rarely bring full retail price. Few, if any, collectors paid the full recommended retail price. The dealers purchase at wholesale and often will sell at little or no profit after a period of time to put the money back into their business.

Hum No. 7 *Merry Wanderer,* $330-$25,000

Hum No.	Basic Size	Trademark	Current Value
7/0	6-1/4"	TMK-1	$750-$1000
7/0	6-1/4"	TMK-2	$475-$650
7/0	6-1/4"	TMK-3	$430-$455
7/0	6-1/4"	TMK-4	$375-$410
7/0	6-1/4"	TMK-5	$350-$370
7/0	6-1/4"	TMK-6	$335-$340
7/0	6-1/4"	TMK-7	$330-$335
7/0	6-1/4"	TMK-8	$330
7/I (double step base)	7"	TMK-1	$1510-$1750
7/I (double step base)	7"	TMK-2	$1310-$1500
7/I (doublestep base)	7"	TMK-3	$1210-$1300
7/I (plain base)	7"	TMK-3	$600-$750
7/I	7"	TMK-4	$500-$600
7/I	7"	TMK-5	$475-$500
7/I	7"	TMK-6	$450-$475
7/I	7"	TMK-7	$425-$450
7/II	9-1/2"	TMK-1	$3000-$3500
7/II	9-1/2"	TMK-2	$1900-$2750

Hum No.	Basic Size	Trademark	Current Value
7/II	9-1/2"	TMK-3	$1700-$1800
7/II	9-1/2"	TMK-4	$1500-$1700
7/II	9-1/2"	TMK-5	$1250-$1275
7/II	9-1/2"	TMK-6	$1225-$1250
7/II	9-1/2"	TMK-7	$1200-$1225
7/III	11-1/4"	TMK-1	$3300-$4000
7/III	11-1/4"	TMK-2	$2500-$3000
7/III	11-1/4"	TMK-3	$1700-$2000
7/III	11-1/4"	TMK-4	$1400-$1500
7/III	11-1/4"	TMK-5	$1300-$1350
7/III	11-1/4"	TMK-6	$1250-$1300
7/X	32"	TMK-5	$20,000-$25,750
7/X	32"	TMK-6	$15,000-$25,750
7/X	32"	TMK-7	$15,000-$25,750
7/X	32"	TMK-8	$15,000-$25,750

Hum No. 8 *Book Worm,* $255-$850

Hum 8: Book Worm

This figure is the same as Hum 3, except much smaller. First modeled by master sculptor Reinhold Unger in 1935, it was one of the original 46 to be offered at the Leipzig Fair that same year. It is found in only one size and remains in production today. At least one terra cotta *Book Worm* is known to be in collectors' hands, and if one exists, more may be out there.

Hum No.	Basic Size	Trademark	Current Value
8	4"	TMK-1	$700-$850
8	4"	TMK-2	$425-$500
8	4"	TMK-3	$350-$400
8	4"	TMK-4	$325-$350
8	4"	TMK-5	$290-$300
8	4"	TMK-6	$270-$290
8	4"	TMK-7	$255-$260
8	4"	TMK-8	$255

Hum 9: Begging His Share

There are two notable variations of this piece. Although originally designed by master sculptor Arthur Moeller in 1935 to be a candleholder, until 1964, it can be found with and without the candle-holding hole in the cake. In 1964, the hole was eliminated when the figurine was remodeled. The Stylized Bee (TMK-3) pieces seem to be those found most often without the hole. The Crown Mark (TMK-1) is the rarest occurrence of the no-hole variation.

Although not a major variation in terms of value, the fact that the earliest of the TMK-1 pieces have brightly colored striped socks is worth mentioning. Also, the earliest of these are the ones more likely to be found without the hole in the cake.

A very rare variation is illustrated by the left figure in the photo here. This no-base, large-shoes figure may have been intended to be utilized as a bookend piece, or it may have been simply an experiment. Whatever the case, if found it would command a low five-figure sum.

The piece was temporarily withdrawn in January 1999.

Hum No.	Basic Size	Trademark	Current Value
9	5-1/2"	TMK-1	$750-$900

Hum No.	Basic Size	Trademark	Current Value
9	5-1/2"	TMK-2	$450-$600
9 (hole)	5-1/2"	TMK-3	$400-$450
9 (without hole)	5-1/2"	TMK-3	$350-$400
9	5-1/2"	TMK-4	$325-$350
9	5-1/2"	TMK-5	$300-$325
9	5-1/2"	TMK-6	$290-$300
9	5-1/2"	TMK-7	$280-$290

Hum 10: Flower Madonna

Created in 1935 by master sculptor Reinhold Unger, this piece was listed in early catalogs as *"Virgin With Flowers"* and *"Sitting Madonna with Child."*

Several color and mold variations are known for this figure. In both sizes, it appears in color and in white overglaze. There have been reports of the figure occurring in tan, beige or brown, and in a royal blue, as well as in terra cotta in 10/III (13") and in 10/I size (9-1/2") with the Crown Mark (TMK-1).

The Crown Mark pieces all have the open-style or "doughnut" type halo. The figure was remodeled in the mid-1950s, eliminating the hole in the halo (closed halo). Because this took place during a

Hum No. 9 *Begging His Share*, $280-$900

trademark transition from the Crown to the Full Bee marks, the Full Bee figures (TMK-2) are the pieces in which both types of halos are found. The Full Bee pieces with open halo bring about 20% more than those with closed halos. This variation has no significant influence on the white overglaze pieces.

The values of the significantly early color variations are $2500 to $3000 for the 10/I size and $3000 to $3500 for the 10/III size.

In 1996, the 50th anniversary of M.I. Hummel's death, Goebel issued a special edition of this piece in the 8-1/4" size for $225. The figure was on a hardwood base with a brass plaque.

Both the 10/I and 10/III sizes were temporarily withdrawn during TMK-6 period.

Hum No.	Basic Size	Trademark	Current Value
10/I (white)	9-1/2"	TMK-1	$500-$600
10/I (white)	9-1/2"	TMK-2	$300-$475
10/I (white)	8-1/4"	TMK-3	$275-$300
10/I (white)	8-1/4"	TMK-5	$230-$255
10/I (color)	9-1/2"	TMK-1	$800-$950
10/I (color)	9-1/2"	TMK-2	$700-$800
10/I (color)	8-1/4"	TMK-3	$575-$675
10/I (color)	8-1/4"	TMK-5	$500-$525

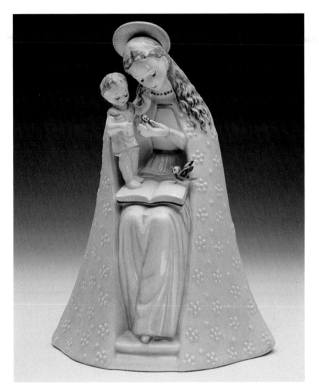

Hum No. 10 *Flower Madonna,* $230-$950

Hum No.	Basic Size	Trademark	Current Value
10/I (color)	8-1/4"	TMK-6	$475-$500
10/III (white)	13"	TMK-1	$450-$750
10/III (white) open halo	13"	TMK-2	$450-$650
10/III (white) closed halo	13"	TMK-2	$450-$650
10/III (white)	11-1/2"	TMK-3	$400-$470
10/III (white)	11-1/2"	TMK-5	$325-$350
10/III (white)	11-1/2"	TMK-6	$300-$325
10/III (color) open halo	13"	TMK-2	$800-$900
10/III (color) closed halo	13"	TMK-2	$800-$900
10/III (color)	11-1/2"	TMK-3	$600-$650
10/III (color)	11-1/2"	TMK-5	$525-$550
10/III (color)	11-1/2"	TMK-6	$500-$525

Hum No. 11 *Merry Wanderer*, $165-$750

Hum 11: Merry Wanderer

This is the same design as the Hum 7, *Merry Wanderer*, and it too was first modeled by master sculptor Arthur Moeller in 1935.

Although most of these figures have five buttons on their vest, there are six- and seven-button versions of the 11/2/0 size. These bring a bit more than the five-button version of the 11/2/0 size, but it is not significant (about 10%).

The Hum 11 model of the *Merry Wanderer* has been found with faience finish.

In 1993, as part of a special Disneyland and Disney World promotion, an unknown number of the small *Merry Wanderers* were given a special decal transfer mark beneath the base to commemorate the occasion. The piece was supposed to be sold along with a similar-sized limited-edition Mickey Mouse. The Mickey Mouse has an incised mold number of 17322, a limited-edition indicator, and TMK-7. The *Merry Wanderer* is a regular production 11/2/0.

The problem was that the *Merry Wanderers* did not make it to the theme parks in time for the promotion. The edition for the pair on a wooden base was 1,500. The first sales of them on the secondary market apparently took place at the site of the M.I. Hummel Club Member Convention in

Milwaukee, Wisconsin, in May 1993. Some private individuals were selling the figures out of their hotel room for $650 per set. They have been advertised for as high as $1000 since then.

Hum No.	Basic Size	Trademark	Current Value
11	4-3/4"	TMK-1	$600-$750
11/2/0	4-1/4"	TMK-1	$450-$550
11/2/0	4-1/4"	TMK-2	$250-$325
11/2/0	4-1/4"	TMK-3	$225-$250
11/2/0	4-1/4"	TMK-4	$190-$225
11/2/0	4-1/4"	TMK-5	$175-$190
11/2/0	4-1/4"	TMK-6	$170-$175
11/2/0	4-1/4"	TMK-7	$165-$170
11/2/0	4-1/4"	TMK-8	$170
11/0	4-3/4"	TMK-1	$550-$700
11/0	4-3/4"	TMK-2	$400-$500
11/0	4-3/4"	TMK-3	$325-$375
11/0	4-3/4"	TMK-4	$300-$325
11/0	4-3/4"	TMK-5	$275-$300
11/0	4-3/4"	TMK-6	$250-$275
11/0	4-3/4"	TMK-7	$225-$230

Hum 12: Chimney Sweep

When first introduced in 1935 as part of the original group displayed at the Leipzig Fair, this figure was called "*Smoky.*" It was first designed by master sculptor Arthur Moeller in 1935 with several restylings through the years.

The small 4" size was not added to the line until well into the 1950s, and consequently, no Crown Mark (TMK-1) pieces are found in that size. There are many variations in size, but none are significant. Examples found in sales lists are 4", 5-1/2", 6-1/4", and 6-3/8".

There was a surprise in store for those who bought the 1992 Sampler (a Hummel introductory kit). In it was the usual club membership discount and that year's figurine, *Chimney Sweep.* Along with the figure came a special display base of a rooftop and chimney.

In 1995, Goebel produced for German retail promotion a special edition of the *Chimney Sweep* with a gilded base. The edition was limited to 500 pieces.

Hum No.	Basic Size	Trademark	Current Value
12/2/0	4"	TMK-2	$250-$325
12/2/0	4"	TMK-3	$175-$200

Hum No. 12 *Chimney Sweep*, $145-$850

Hum No.	Basic Size	Trademark	Current Value
12/2/0	4"	TMK-4	$160-$175
12/2/0	4"	TMK-5	$150-$160
12/2/0	4"	TMK-6	$145-$150
12	5-1/2"	TMK-1	$700-$850
12	5-1/2"	TMK-2	$425-$500
12/I	5-1/2"	TMK-1	$700-$850
12/I	5-1/2"	TMK-2	$425-$500
12/I	5-1/2"	TMK-3	$350-$410
12/I	5-1/2"	TMK-4	$325-$350
12/I	5-1/2"	TMK-5	$270-$300
12/I	5-1/2"	TMK-6	$260-$270
12/I	5-1/2"	TMK-7	$255-$260
12/I	5-1/2"	TMK-8	$260

Hum 13: Meditation

The Hum 13/0 and the Hum 13/II sizes were the first to be released in 1935 and were first modeled by Reinhold Unger.

The most significant variations are with regard to the flowers in the baskets. When first released, the 13/II had flowers in the basket, but sometime in the Last Bee (TMK-5) era, the piece was restyled by master sculptor Gerhard Skrobek to reflect no flowers in the basket, and the style remains so today.

Variations in the Hum 13/0 are with regard to the pigtails. The first models of the figure in the Crown Mark (TMK-1) era sported short pigtails with a painted red ribbon. By the time the Full Bee (TMK-2) was being utilized, the ribbon had disappeared and the pigtails had grown longer.

The larger Hum 13/V was copyrighted in 1957 and has a basket filled with flowers. It is scarce in the older trademarks and hardly ever found for sale. It was temporarily withdrawn from production on December 31, 1989. Also temporarily withdrawn were 13/2/0 and 13/0 pieces in January 1999.

There is a very unusual and probably unique *Meditation* that has a bowl attached to its side. There have been three different figurines found with bowls attached. The other two are *Goose Girl* and *Congratulations*.

Hum No. 13 *Meditation,* $160-$5000

Hum No.	Basic Size	Trademark	Current Value
13/2/0	4-1/4"	TMK-2	$250-$350
13/2/0	4-1/4"	TMK-3	$225-$250
13/2/0	4-1/4"	TMK-4	$190-$225
13/2/0	4-1/4"	TMK-5	$175-$190
13/2/0	4-1/4"	TMK-6	$160-$170
13/0	5-1/4"	TMK-1	$700-$850
13/0	6"	TMK-2	$425-$500
13/0	5-1/4"	TMK-3	$350-$400
13/0	5"	TMK-4	$325-$350
13/0	5"	TMK-5	$270-$300
13/0	5"	TMK-6	$260-$270
13/0	5"	TMK-7	$245-$260
13/II (13/2) with flowers	7"	TMK-1	$4000-$5000
13/II (13/2) with flowers	7"	TMK-2	$3500-$4000
13/II (13/2) with flowers	7"	TMK-3	$3000-$3500
13/II	7"	TMK-5	$410-$455
13/II	7"	TMK-6	$350-$410
13/V	13-3/4"	TMK-1	$4000-$5,000
13/V	13-3/4"	TMK-2	$3000-$3,500
13/V	13-3/4"	TMK-3	$1700-$2200

Hum No.	Basic Size	Trademark	Current Value
13/V	13-3/4"	TMK-4	$1350-$1500
13/V	13-3/4"	TMK-5	$1300-$1350
13/V	13-3/4"	TMK-6	$1200-$1300

Hum 14/A and Hum 14/B: Book Worms (Bookends)

These are two figures, a boy and a girl (see Hum 3 and Hum 8). As far as is known to date, there is no other occurrence of the boy *Book Worm* anywhere else in the collection. It occurs only in conjunction with the bookends (Hum 14/A and Hum 14/B) in only one size. Early marketed boy pieces were titled "*Learned Man*."

These bookends do not have wooden bases. (Other bookends in the collection typically do have wooden bases.) There are holes on the bottom where the figures are weighted with sand, etc., and usually sealed with cork, a plastic plug, or a factory sticker, gold in color.

These bookends were temporarily withdrawn on December 31, 1989, but in 1993, they could be purchased by mail-order from Danbury Mint, thus the existence of the TMK-7 pieces.

Fakes and Forgeries

Be on the lookout for imitation Hummel pieces.
The quality of these pieces ranges, but none
are able to completely capture the essence
of a true Hummel. For more information
on detecting fakes see page 46.

**Hum No. 14/A and 14/B *Book Worms* (Bookends),
$400-$1600**

Hum No.	Basic Size	Trademark	Current Value
14	5-1/2"	TMK-1	$600-$800
14/A&B	5-1/2"	TMK-1	$1200-$1600
14/A&B	5-1/2"	TMK-2	$650-$750
14/A&B	5-1/2"	TMK-3	$600-$650
14/A&B	5-1/2"	TMK-4	$550-$600
14/A&B	5-1/2"	TMK-5	$500-$550
14/A&B	5-1/2"	TMK-6	$450-$500
14/A&B	5-1/2"	TMK-7	$400-$450

Hum 15: Hear Ye, Hear Ye

Among the first 46 to be released by Goebel at the Leipzig Fair, this figure was first called "*Night Watchman*" and remained so until around 1950. It was first modeled by master sculptor Arthur Moeller in 1935.

Serious collectors seek out the larger 7-1/2" size with the Arabic size designator "15/2," for it represents the oldest of Crown Mark (TMK-1) figures and is worth up to $1700.

Also sought-after—but very rare—are a few early samples in the faience style, which are valued at $3000-$5000.

In January 2002, the QVC offered a special 1,000-piece limited edition *Hear Ye! Hear Ye!* Progression Set (Hum 15/0). The set consisted of three figurines—one in whiteware, one partially painted, and one completed—along with a wooden display stand with commemorative porcelain plaque and authentic Goebel painter's brush. *On Holiday* (Hum 350) was offered in the same type of progression set later in the year.

Both the 15/I and 15/II sizes have been temporarily withdrawn, while the 15/0 variation remains in production today.

Hum No.	Basic Size	Trademark	Current Value
15/2/0	4"	TMK-6	$185-$190
15/2/0	4"	TMK-7	$180-$185
15/2/0	4"	TMK-8	$185
15/0	5"	TMK-1	$600-$750
15/0	5"	TMK-2	$350-$450
15/0	5"	TMK-3	$300-$325
15/0	5"	TMK-4	$275-$300
15/0	5"	TMK-5	$250-$270
15/0	5"	TMK-6	$240-$250
15/0	5"	TMK-7	$230-$240
15/0	5"	TMK-8	$240

Hum No. 15 *Hear Ye, Hear Ye,* $180-$900

Hum No.	Basic Size	Trademark	Current Value
15/I	6"	TMK-1	$700-$900
15/I	6"	TMK-2	$450-$600
15/I	6"	TMK-3	$375-$400
15/I	6"	TMK-4	$350-$375
15/I	6"	TMK-5	$310-$340
15/I	6"	TMK-6	$290-$310
15/I	6"	TMK-7	$280-$285
15/II	7-1/2"	TMK-1	$1200-$1500
15/II	7-1/2"	TMK-2	$750-$1000
15/II	7-1/2"	TMK-3	$650-$750
15/II	7-1/2"	TMK-4	$550-$650
15/II	7-1/2"	TMK-5	$500-$525
15/II	7-1/2"	TMK-6	$475-$500
15/II	7-1/2"	TMK-7	$450-$475
15	7-1/2"	TMK-1	$1400-$1700

Hum 16: Little Hiker

Modeled by master sculptor Arthur Moeller, *Little Hiker* is one of the original 46 released in the 16/I and 16/2/0 sizes and was originally referred to as "*Happy-Go-Lucky.*"

The only significant variation is with the mold number. The mold number is sometimes found with only the 16 and sometimes with the decimal designator "16." in the 5-1/2" to 6" size. These are found with the Crown (TMK-1) and the Full Bee (TMK-2) trademarks and will bring about 15% more than comparably trademarked 16/I figures.

Early painting samples have been found with a green jacket and blue hat. These are worth $1500-$2000. And if found with an attached pot as shown in an old company product book, the piece would be worth $5000-$10,000.

The 16/I size has been temporarily withdrawn from production, and the 16/2/0 variation was permanently retired on December 31, 2002. Those made in 2002 bear a "Final Issue 2002" backstamp and came with a "Final Issue" medallion.

Hum No.	Basic Size	Trademark	Current Value
16/2/0	4-1/4"	TMK-1	$350-$450
16/2/0	4-1/4"	TMK-2	$250-$300

Hum No. 16 *Little Hiker,* $140-$700

Hum No.	Basic Size	Trademark	Current Value
16/2/0	4-1/4"	TMK-3	$175-$200
16/2/0	4-1/4"	TMK-4	$160-$175
16/2/0	4-1/4"	TMK-5	$150-$160
16/2/0	4-1/4"	TMK-6	$145-$150
16/2/0	4-1/4"	TMK-7	$140-$145
16/2/0	4-1/4"	TMK-8	$145
16/I	5-1/2"	TMK-1	$600-$700
16/I	5-1/2"	TMK-2	$400-$500
16/I	5-1/2"	TMK-3	$350-$400
16/I	5-1/2"	TMK-4	$300-$350
16/I	5-1/2"	TMK-5	$275-$300
16/I	5-1/2"	TMK-6	$260-$275
16/I	5-1/2"	TMK-7	$245-$250

Hum 17: Congratulations

One of the original 1935 releases, *Congratulations* was first modeled by master sculptor Reinhold Unger.

There is a very unusual, perhaps unique, version of this piece where a bowl is attached to the figurine's right rear. The figurine in this version does not have the normal base.

When first modeled, the girl had no socks. Later versions (after 1970) have a new hairstyle that appears to be a little longer. The flowers in the pot are larger, and the girl wears socks. This change was made during the Three Line Mark (TMK-4) and Stylized Bee (TMK-5) eras, so you can find either version with these marks. Obviously, the no-socks piece would be the more desirable one.

Once again, an early product book shows a sample with an attached pot. If found, that piece is worth $5000-$10,000.

The final issue of this figurine was produced in 1999.

Hum No.	Basic Size	Trademark	Current Value
17/0 (no socks)	6"	TMK-1	$600-$750

Hum No. 17 *Congratulations*, $240-$8000

Hum No.	Basic Size	Trademark	Current Value
17/0 (no socks)	6"	TMK-2	$350-$450
17/0 (no socks)	6"	TMK-3	$300-$325
17/0 (no socks)	6"	TMK-4	$275-$300
17/0 (socks)	6"	TMK-5	$250-$275
17/0 (socks)	6"	TMK-6	$240-$250
17/0	6"	TMK-7	$230-$235
17/2 or 17/II	8-1/4"	TMK-1	$6500-$8000
17/2 or 17/II	8-1/4"	TMK-2	$5500-$6500
17/2 or 17/II	8-1/4"	TMK-3	$4500-$5500

Price Guide

Price ranges may reflect various demands in the market from one geographic region to another; condition of piece; specific marking found on piece; and/or changes in production of piece.

*= date unknown

Figurines

	Year	Price
Bavarian Village Collection		
Happy Pastime Hum 69	1996	**$190-$650**
Century Collection		
Fanfare Hum 1999	1999	**N/A**
Love's Bounty Hum 751	1996	**$1600-$1800**
Pleasant Journey Hum 406	1987	**$2750-$3000**
Strike Up The Band Hum 668	1995	**$1400-$1600**

Due to space constraints, a range of pricing has been provided in some instances. Please consult the 12th edition of Luckey's Hummel® Figurines & Plates Identification and Price Guide *for individual pricing based upon trademark variations.*

	Year	Price
Club Exclusive		
At Grandpa's Hum 621	1996	**$1500-$1600**
Country Suitor Hum 760	1995	**$195-$225**
Club Exclusive		
Strum Along Hum 557	1995	**$155**
M.I. Hummel		
A Fair Measure Hum 345	1972	**$350-$5000**
Accompanist, The Hum 453	1988	**$140**
Accordion Boy Hum 185	1947	**$200-$750**
Adoration Hum 23	*	**$1600-$2100**
Adoration Hum 23/I	*	**$430-$1400**
Adoration Hum 23/III	*	**$595-$2000**
Adoration With Bird, Hum 105	1938	**$7000-$8000**
Adventure Bound Hum 347	1971	**$4350-$15000**
An Apple A Day Hum 403	1989	**$350-$4000**
Angel Duet Hum 261	1968	**$270-$850**
Angel Duet, Candleholder Hum 193	*	**$250-$1800**
Angel Lights, Candleholder Hum 241	*	**$300-$500**
Angel Serendade Hum 83	*	**$270-$750**
Angel With Accordion Hum 238 B	1967	**$73-$125**
Angel With Lute Hum 238 A	1967	**$73-$125**

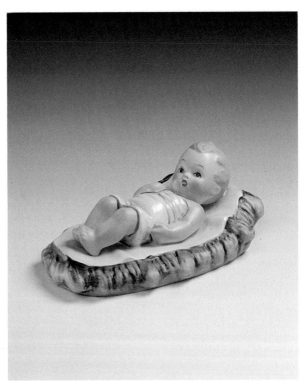

Hum No. 18 *Christ Child*, $165-$550

Hum No. 21 *Heavenly Angel*, **$160-1600**

Hum No. 23/I *Adoration*, $430-$1400

	Year	Price
M.I. Hummel		
Angel With Trumpet		
Hum 238 C	1967	$73-$125
Angel/Accordion, Candleholder		
Hum 1/39/0	*	$80-$200
Angel/Accordion, Candleholder		
Hum 111/39/0	*	$60-$200
Angel/Accordion, Candleholder		
Hum 111/39/1	*	$200-$350
Angel/Lute, Candleholder		
Hum 1/38/0	*	$73-$200
Angel/Lute, Candleholder		
Hum 111/38/0	*	$80-$200
Angel/Lute, Candleholder		
Hum 111/38/1	*	$200-$350
Angel/Trumpet, Candleholder		
Hum 1/40/0	*	$73-$200
Angel/Trumpet, Candleholder		
Hum 111/40/0	*	$60-$200
Angel/Trumpet, Candleholder		
Hum 111/40/1	*	$200-$350
Angel/Two Children At		
Feet Hum 108	*	$2500-$15,000
Angelic Conductor		
Hum 2096/A	2002	$135
Angelic Sleep, Candleholder		
Hum 25	*	$200-$2000

Hum No. 27 *Joyous News*, $250-$2000

Hum No. 32 *Little Gabriel*, $180-$2500

	Year	Price
M.I. Hummel		
Angelic Song Hum 144	*	$185-$550
Angler, The Hum 566	1995	$395
Angler, The Hum 566	1995	$400-$595
Apple Tree Boy Hum 142	*	$650-$950
Apple Tree Boy Hum 142/3/0	*	$180-$550
Apple Tree Boy Hum 142/I	*	$350-$800
Apple Tree Boy Hum 142/V	*	$1495-$2000
Apple Tree Boy Hum 142/X	*	$26,500-$30,000
Apple Tree Boy, Candleholder Hum 677	*	$200-$250
Apple Tree Boy, Table Lamp Hum 230	*	$375-$1000
Apple Tree Boy/Girl-Bookends Hum 252 A&B	*	$300-$425
Apple Tree Girl Hum 141	*	$650-$950
Apple Tree Girl Hum 141/3/0	*	$180-$550
Apple Tree Girl Hum 141/I	*	$350-$800
Apple Tree Girl Hum 141/V	*	$1495-$1700
Apple Tree Girl Hum 141/X	*	$26,000-$26,550

Due to space constraints, a range of pricing has been provided in some instances. Please consult the 12th edition of Luckey's Hummel® Figurines & Plates Identification and Price Guide for individual pricing based upon trademark variations.

Hum No. 36/0 *Holy Water Font,*
Child With Flowers, **$58-$300**

	Year	Price

M.I. Hummel

	Year	Price
Apple Tree Girl, Candleholder Hum 676	*	**$200-$250**
Apple Tree Girl, Table Lamp Hum 229	*	**$375-$1000**
Art Critic Hum 318	1991	**$315-$5000**
Artist Hum 304	*	**$305-$5000**
Auf Wiedersehen Hum 153	*	**$650-$1200**
Auf Wiedersehen Hum 153/I	*	**$340-$1050**
Auf Wiedersehen Hum 153/0	*	**$285-$4000**
Authorized Retailer Plaque Hum 460	*	**$200-$1500**
Autumn Harvest Hum 355	*	**$250-$3000**
Ba-Bee-Ring 30/0 A&B Red	*	**$6000-$7000**
Ba-Bee-Ring 30/I A&B Red	*	**$8000-$9000**
Ba-Bee-Ring Hum 30/0 A&B	*	**$245-$700**
Baker Hum 128	*	**$250-$750**
Baking Day Hum 330	1985	**$250-$5000**
Band Leader Hum 129	*	**$260-$750**
Band Leader Hum 129/4/0	*	**$125-$140**
Barnyard Hero Hum 195	*	**$650-$1200**
Barnyard Hero Hum 195/2/0	*	**$205-$450**
Barnyard Hero Hum 195/I	*	**$350-$700**
Bashful Hum 377	*	**$250-$4000**
Bashful Serenade Hum 2133	2002	**$475**
Basket Of Gifts Hum 618	2002	**$375**
Bath Time Hum 412	1990	**$535-$4000**

Hum No. 42 *Good Shepherd*, $280-$8000

Hum No. 47/0 *Goose Girl*, $290-$900

Hum No. 49/3/0 *To Market*, $195-$650

	Year	Price
M.I. Hummel		
Be Mine Hum 2050/B	1999	$95
Be Patient Hum 197	*	$250-$1000
Be Patient Hum 197/2/0	*	$250-$550
Be Patient Hum 197/I	*	$330-$650
Begging His Share Hum 9	*	$280-$900
Big Housecleaning Hum 363	*	$335-$5000
Bird Duet Hum 169	*	$185-$550
Bird Watcher Hum 300	1979	$270-$5000
Birthday Cake, Candleholder Hum 338	1989	$195-$5000
Birthday Present Hum 341	1956	$180-$5000
Birthday Present Hum 341/3/O	1989	$180-$190
Birthday Serenade Hum 218	*	$210-$1500
Birthday Serenade Hum 218/1	*	$1000-$1500
Birthday Serenade Hum 218/2/0	*	$210-$700
Birthday Serenade Hum 218/0	*	$330-$975
Birthday Serenade, Table Lamp Hum 231	*	$500-$3000
Birthday Serenade, Table Lamp Hum 234	*	$425-$2100
Blessed Child (Krumbad) Hum 78/I	*	$30-$50
Blessed Child (Krumbad) Hum 78/II	*	$35-$60

Hum No. 50/0 *Volunteers*, $375-$1100

Hum No. 51/3/0 *Village Boy*, $150-$450

Hum No. 52 *Going To Grandma's*, $305-$1600

	Year	Price
M.I. Hummel		
Blessed Child (Krumbad) Hum 78/II 1/2	*	$75-$150
Blessed Child (Krumbad) Hum 78/III	*	$45-$400
Blessed Child (Krumbad) Hum 78/0	*	$150-$300
Blessed Child (Krumbad) Hum 78/V	*	$80-$150
Blessed Child (Krumbad) Hum 78/VI	*	$150-$850
Blessed Child (Krumbad) Hum 78/VIII	*	$300-$1000
Blessed Event Hum 333	*	$400-$5000
Blossom Time Hum 608	1996	$175
Book Worm Hum 3/I	*	$370-$1110
Book Worm Hum 3/II	*	$1110-$3500
Book Worm Hum 3/III	*	$1250-$4000
Book Worm Hum 8	*	$255-$850
Book Worm Bookends, Boy & Girl Hum 14	*	$600-$800
Book Worm, Bookends, Hum 14 A&B	*	$400-$1600
Boots Hum 143	*	$650-$1050
Boots Hum 143/I	*	$360-$1000
Boots Hum 143/0	*	$225-$700
Botanist Hum 351	1982	$215-$2000

Hum No. 56/A *Culprits*, $365-$650

Hum No. 56B *Out Of Danger*, $345-$650

Hum No. 57/2/0 *Chick Girl*, \$185-\$200

	Year	Price

M.I. Hummel

Boy And Girl, Wall Vase Hum 360 A	1979	$190-$750
Boy Feeding Birds Hum 233	1954	N/A
Boy With Horse, Candlestick Hum 117	*	$73-$275
Boy With Accordion Hum 390	*	$110-$275
Boy With Bird, Ashtray Hum 166	*	$140-$650
Boy With Horse Hum 239 C	*	$73-$200
Boy With Toothache Hum 217	*	$250-$525
Boy, Wall Vase Hum 360 B	1979	$190-$750
Brother Hum 95	*	$250-$800
Budding Maestro Hum 477	1988	$120-$135
Builder Hum 305	*	$305-$5000
Bumblebee Friend Hum 837	2002	$260

Due to space constraints, a range of pricing has been provided in some instances. Please consult the 12th edition of Luckey's Hummel® Figurines & Plates Identification and Price Guide *for individual pricing based upon trademark variations.*

Hum No. 58/2/0 *Playmates*, $185-$200

Hum No. 63 *Singing Lesson*, $155-$550

FINAL ISSUE
LETZTE AUSGABE
1993

Hum No. 65 *Farewell*, $275-$1000

	Year	Price
M.I. Hummel		
Busy Student Hum 367	*	$200-$1100
Call To Glory Hum 739	1994	$295
Candlelight, Candleholder		
Hum 192	*	$270-$1800
Carnival Hum 328	*	$250-$5000
Celestial Drummer		
Hum 2096/C	2002	$135
Celestial Musician (Mini)		
Hum 188/4/0	*	$130-$140
Celestial Musician Hum 188	*	$350-$2000
Celestial Musician Hum 188/I	*	$310-$350
Celestial Musician Hum 188/0	*	$268-$280
Celestial Strings Hum 2096/F	2002	$135
Cheeky Fellow Hum 299	1999	$145
Chick Girl Hum 57	*	$500-$1050
Chick Girl Hum 57/2/0	*	$185-$200
Chick Girl Hum 57/I	*	$310-$1000
Chick Girl Hum 57/0	*	$205-$700
Chick Girl, Candy Box		
(New Style) Hum III-57	*	$300-$350
Chick Girl, Candy Box		
(Old Style) Hum III-57	*	$475-$550
Chicken-Licken Hum 385	*	$350-$1500
Chicken-Licken Hum 385/4/0	*	$115-$140
Child In Bed, Looking		
Left Hum 137 A	*	$5000-$7000

Hum No. 66 *Farm Boy*, $270-$900

Hum No. 67 *Doll Mother,* $257-$900

Hum No. 69 *Happy Pastime*, $190-$650

	Year	**Price**
M.I. Hummel		
Child In Bed, Looking Right Hum 137 B	✼	$80-$550
Child In Bed, Plaque Hum 137	✼	$75
Chimney Sweep Hum 12	✼	$425-$800
Chimney Sweep Hum 12/2/0	✼	$145-$325
Chimney Sweep Hum 12/I	✼	$260-$850
Christ Child Hum 18	✼	$165-$550
Christmas Angel Hum 301	1989	$310-$5000
Christmas Gift	1999	$95
Christmas Song Hum 343	✼	$270-$5000
Christmas Song Hum 343/4/0	1996	$135
Cinderella Hum 337	✼	$355-$5000
Close Harmony Hum 336	✼	$375-$5000
Come Back Soon Hum 545	1995	$180-$500
Confidentially Hum 314	✼	$325-$5000
Congratulations Hum 17/2	✼	$4500-$8000
Congratulations Hum 17/0	✼	$230-$750
Coquettes Hum 179	1948	$325-$1100
Crossroads Hum 331	✼	$510-$5000

Due to space constraints, a range of pricing has been provided in some instances. Please consult the 12th edition of Luckey's Hummel® Figurines & Plates Identification and Price Guide *for individual pricing based upon trademark variations.*

Hum No. 70 *The Holy Child*, $280-$850

Hum No. 71/2/0 *Stormy Weather*, $365-$380

Hum No. 74 *Little Gardner*, $150-$550

	Year	Price
M.I. Hummel		
Cuddles Hum 2049/A	1999	$85-$100
Culprits Hum 56	*	$900-$1100
Culprits Hum 56 A	*	$365-$650
Culprits, Table Lamp Hum 44	*	$650-$750
Culprits, Table Lamp Hum 44 A	*	$325-$650
Cymbals Of Joy Hum 2096/U	2002	$140
Daddy's Girls Hum 371	1989	$275-$4000
Dearly Beloved Hum 2003	1999	$200-$520
Delicious Hum 435	1996	$175-$3000
Delicious Hum 435/3/0		$170-$175
Divine Drummer Hum 2096/M	2002	$135
Doctor Hum 127	*	$190-$650
Doll Bath Hum 319	*	$355-$5000
Doll Mother Hum 67	*	$257-$900
Doll Mother/Prayer.. Bkends Hum 76 A&B	*	$10,000-$15,000
Duet (With "Lips" Base) Hum 130	*	$300-$1500

Due to space constraints, a range of pricing has been provided in some instances. Please consult the 12th edition of Luckey's Hummel® Figurines & Plates Identification and Price Guide *for individual pricing based upon trademark variations.*

Hum No. 80 *Little Scholar*, $270-$800

Hum No. 84/V *Worship*, $1125-$3000

Hum No. 87 *For Father*, $270-$800

	Year	**Price**
M.I. Hummel		
Duet (Without Ties), Hum 130	*	**$3500**
Duet Hum 130	*	**$300-$1000**
Easter Greetings! Hum 378	*	**$225-$4000**
Easter Time Hum 384	1972	**$300-$1500**
Evening Prayer Hum 495	1991	**$135**
Eventide (Rare) Hum 99	*	**$3000-$3500**
Eventide Hum 99	*	**$360-$1250**
Eventide, Table Lamp Hum 104	*	**$8000-$10,000**
Extra! Extra! Hum 2113	2002	**$240**
Farewell Hum 65	*	**$275-$1000**
Farewell Hum 65/I	*	**$325-$1000**
Farewell Hum 65/0	*	**$5000-$8000**
Farewell, Table Lamp Hum 103	*	**$8000-$10,000**
Farm Boy Hum 66	*	**$270-$900**
Farm Boy/Goose Girl Bookends Hum 60 A&B	*	**$400-$1250**
Favorite Pet Hum 361	*	**$335-$5000**
Feathered Friends Hum 344	*	**$350-$1000**
Feeding Time Hum 199	*	**$525-$1000**
Feeding Time Hum 199/I	*	**$315-$575**
Feeding Time Hum 199/0	*	**$250-$500**
Festival Harmony (Flute) Hum 173	*	**$1000-$3500**
Festival Harmony (Flute) Hum 173/4/0	*	**$130**

Hum No. 88/I *Heavenly Protection*, $540-$750

Hum No. 89 *Little Cellist*, $1250-$1600

Hum No. 94/3/0 *Surprise*, $190-$550

	Year	Price
M.I. Hummel		
Festival Harmony		
(Flute) Hum 173/II	*	**$450-$800**
Festival Harmony (Flute)		
Hum 173/0	*	**$350-$650**
Festival Harmony		
(Mandolin) Hum 172	*	**$1000-$3500**
Festival Harmony		
(Mandolin) Hum 172/4/0	*	**$135**
Festival Harmony		
(Mandolin) Hum 172/II	*	**$450-$800**
Festival Harmony		
(Mandolin) Hum 172/0	*	**$350-$650**
First Bloom	2000	**$95**
Flitting Butterfly,		
Plaque Hum 139	*	**$75-$550**
Flower For You, A	2000	**$95**
Flower Vendor Hum 381	*	**$305-$4000**
Flying Angel Hum 366	*	**$150-$275**
Flying High Hum 452	1984	**$175-$300**

Due to space constraints, a range of pricing has been provided in some instances. Please consult the 12th edition of Luckey's Hummel® Figurines & Plates Identification and Price Guide *for individual pricing based upon trademark variations.*

Hum No. 95 *Brother*, $250-$800

Hum No. 96 *Little Shopper*, $180-$550

Hum No. 98/2/0 *Sister*, $180-$250

	Year	Price
M.I. Hummel		
Follow The Leader Hum 369	*	$1390-$5000
For Father Hum 87	*	$270-$800
For Mother Gift Set		
Hum 257/2/0	1999	$160
For Mother Hum 257	*	$260-$825
For Mother Hum 257/2/0	*	$155
For Mother Hum 257/0	*	$255
Forest Shrine Hum 183	*	$595-$1900
Free Flight Hum 569	1993	$215
Friend Or Foe Hum 434	1991	$275
Friends Hum 136	*	$3000-$15,000
Friends Hum 136/I	*	$240-$950
Friends Hum 136/V	*	$1350-$4000
Frosty Friends Collector's Set	1999	$598
Gay Adventure Hum 356	*	$245-$3000
Gentle Glow, Candleholder		
Hum 439	1987	$238
Girl Playing A Mandolin		
Hum 254	*	N/A
Girl Standing Hands In		
Pockets Hum 161	1943	N/A
Girl Standing Tiered Dress/		
Flowers, Hum 160	1943	N/A
Girl Standing With		
Dog In Arms Hum 158	1943	N/A

Hum No. 99 *Eventide*, $360-$1250

Hum No. 110/I *Let's Sing*, $195-$375

Hum No. 111/I *Wayside Harmony*, **$320**

	Year	Price
M.I. Hummel		
Girl Standing With Flowers		
In Arms, Hum 159	1943	N/A
Girl Standing With		
Handbag Hum 162	1946	N/A
Girl With Accordion Hum 259	1962	$5000-$10,000
Girl With Basket Hum 253	*	N/A
Girl With Fir Tree,		
Candlestick Hum 116	*	$73-$275
Girl With Nosegay,		
Candlestick Hum 115	*	$75-$275
Girl With Doll Hum 239 B	*	$73-$200
Girl With Nosegay Hum 239 A	*	$73-$200
Girl With Sheet Of		
Music Hum 389	*	$110-$275
Girl With Trumpet Hum 391	*	$110-$275
Girl, Wall Vase Hum 360 C	1979	$190-$750
Globe Trotter Hum 79	*	$200-$750
Going Home Hum 383	1985	$395-$4000
Going To Grandma's Hum 52	*	$850-$1600
Going To Grandma's		
Hum 52/I	*	$400-$1500
Going To Grandma's		
Hum 52/0	*	$305-$320
Good Friends Hum 182	*	$250-$750
Good Friends, Bookends		
Hum 251 A&B	*	$300-$750

Hum No. 123 *Max and Moritz*, $270-$800

Hum No. 124/0 *Hello*, $255-$450

Hum No. 127 *Doctor*, $190-$650

	Year	Price
M.I. Hummel		
Good Friends, Candleholder		
Hum 679	1990	$200-$250
Good Friends, Table Lamp		
Hum 228	*	$375-$850
Good Hunting Hum 307	*	$300-$5000
Good Luck Charm Hum 2034	2002	$190
Good Shepherd Hum 42/I	*	$5000-$8000
Good Shepherd Hum 42/0	*	$280-$900
Goose Girl Ann. Clock		
Hum 750	1995	$225
Goose Girl Hum 47	1996	$205-$1300
Goose Girl Hum 47	*	$800-$900
Goose Girl Hum 47/3/0	*	$205-$900
Goose Girl Hum 47/II	*	$400-$1300
Goose Girl Hum 47/0	*	$290-$900
Grandma's Girl Hum 561	1990	$185
Grandpa's Boy Hum 562	1990	$185
Guardian, The Hum 455	1991	$205
Guiding Angel Hum 357	*	$110-$150
Happiness Hum 86	*	$170-$500
Happy Birthday Hum 176	*	$600-$1150
Happy Birthday Hum 176/I	*	$330-$1100
Happy Birthday Hum 176/0	*	$280-$500
Happy Days Hum 150	*	$900-$1600
Happy Days Hum 150/2/0	*	$210-$400
Happy Days Hum 150/I	*	$500-$1550

Hum No. 128 *Baker*, $250-$750

Hum No. 131 *Street Singer*, $245-$700

Hum No. 136 *Friends*, $240-$15,000

	Year	Price
M.I. Hummel		
Happy Days Hum 150/0	*	$330-$625
Happy Days, Table Lamp Hum 232	*	$500-$1700
Happy Days, Table Lamp Hum 235	*	$450-$1100
Happy Pastime Hum 69	*	$190-$650
Happy Pastime, Ashtray Hum 62	*	$150-$650
Happy Pastime, Box (New Style) Hum III/69	*	$200-$350
Happy Pastime, Box (Old Style) Hum III/69	*	$475-$850
Happy Pastime/Candy Jar Hum 221	1952	$5000-$10,000
Happy Traveller Hum 109	*	$1500
Happy Traveller Hum 109	*	$180-$250
Happy Traveller Hum 109/II	*	$375-$900
Happy Traveller Hum 109/0	*	$185-$350
Hear Ye, Hear Ye Hum 15	*	$1400-$1700

Due to space constraints, a range of pricing has been provided in some instances. Please consult the 12th edition of Luckey's Hummel® Figurines & Plates Identification and Price Guide *for individual pricing based upon trademark variations.*

Hum No. 142/3/0 *Apple Tree Boy*, $180-$550

Hum No. 143 *Boots*, $225-$1050

Hum No. 146 *Holy Water Font, Angel Duet*, $60-$225

	Year	Price

M.I. Hummel

	Year	Price
Hear Ye, Hear Ye Hum 15/2/0	*	**$185-$190**
Hear Ye, Hear Ye Hum 15/I	*	**$280-$900**
Hear Ye, Hear Ye Hum 15/II	*	**$450-$1500**
Hear Ye, Hear Ye Hum 15/0	*	**$230-$750**
Heavenly Angel Hum 21/I	*	**$320-$1000**
Heavenly Angel Hum 21/II	*	**$425-$1600**
Heavenly Angel Hum 21/0	*	**$160-$500**
Heavenly Angel Hum 21/0 1/2	*	**$270-$850**
Heavenly Angel Tree Topper Hum 755	1994	**$475-$500**
Heavenly Harmony Hum 2096/L	2002	**$135**
Heavenly Hornplayer Hum 2096/J	2002	**$135**
Heavenly Hubbub Hum 2096/P	2002	**$135**
Heavenly Lullaby Hum 262	*	**$270-$850**
Heavenly Prayer Hum 815	1999	**$195**
Heavenly Protection Hum 88	*	**$1300-$2400**
Heavenly Protection Hum 88/I	*	**$540-$750**
Heavenly Protection Hum 88/II	*	**$800-$1300**
Heavenly Rhapsody Hum 2096/E	2002	**$135**
Heavenly Song, Candleholder, Hum 113	*	**$3000-$10,000**
Hello Hum 124	*	**$450-$1000**

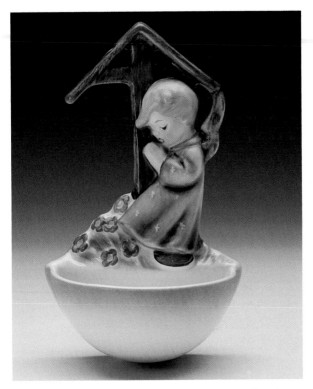

Hum No. 147 *Holy Water Font, Angel Shrine*, $68-$275

Hum No. 150/2/0 *Happy Days*, $210-$400

Hum No. 151/11 *Madonna Holding Child, Blue*, $900-$3000

	Year	Price

M.I. Hummel

	Year	Price
Hello Hum 124/I	*	$275-$1000
Hello Hum 124/0	*	$255-$450
Herald Angels, Candleholder		
Hum 37	*	$180-$800
Holy Child Hum 70	*	$280-$850
Holy Water Font, Angel Cloud		
Hum 206	*	$60-$500
Holy Water Font, Angel		
Duet Hum 146	*	$60-$225
Holy Water Font, Angel		
Joyous News Hum 241	1955	$1500-$2000
Holy Water Font, Angel		
Joyous News Hum 242	1955	$1500-$2000
Holy Water Font, Angel		
Shrine Hum 147	*	$68-$275
Holy Water Font,		
Angel Sitting Hum 22	*	$68-$300
Holy Water Font, Angel		
With Bird Hum 167	*	$300-$325
Holy Water Font, Angel		
With Bird Hum 354C	*	N/A
Holy Water Font, Angel		
With Lantern Hum 354A	*	N/A
Holy Water Font, Angel		
With Trumpet	*	N/A

Hum No. 152/A/0 *Umbrella Boy*, $300

Hum No. 153/0 *Auf Wiedersehen*, $285-$4000

Hum No. 154 *Waiter*, $270-$1150

	Year	Price
M.I. Hummel		
Holy Water Font, Angel/Prayer Hum 91 A&B	*	$115-$500
Holy Water Font, Child Jesus Hum 26	*	$350-$550
Holy Water Font, Child Jesus Hum 26/I	*	$200-$550
Holy Water Font, Child Jesus Hum 26/0	*	$50-$275
Holy Water Font, Child With Flowers Hum 36	*	$400-$450
Holy Water Font, Child/Flowers Hum 36/I	*	$175-$450
Holy Water Font, Child/Flowers Hum 36/0	*	$58-$300
Holy Water Font, Cross With Doves Hum 77	*	$5000-$10,000
Holy Water Font, Good Shepherd Hum 35	*	$400-$450
Holy Water Font, Good Shepherd Hum 35/I	*	$175-$450
Holy Water Font, Good Shepherd Hum 35/0	*	$58-$300
Holy Water Font, Guard. Angel Hum 248/I	*	$1000-$1500
Holy Water Font, Guard. Angel Hum 248/0	*	$62-$250

Hum No. 163 *Whitsuntide*, $330-$1200

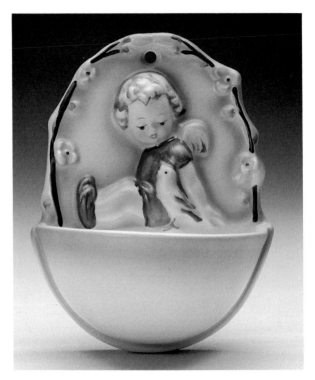

**Hum No. 167 *Holy Water Font,
Angel With Bird*, $300-$325**

Hum No. 169 *Bird Duet*, $185-$550

	Year	Price
M.I. Hummel		
Holy Water Font, Guardian Angel Hum 29/0	*	$950-$1500
Holy Water Font, Guardian Angel Hum 29/I	*	$1500-$2000
Holy Water Font, Guardian Angel Hum 29	*	$1300-$1500
Holy Water Font, Heavenly Angel Hum 207	*	$85-$500
Holy Water Font, Holy Family Hum 246	*	$68-$300
Holy Water Font, Madonna With Child Hum 243	*	$68-$300
Holy Water Font, White Angel Hum 75	*	$45-$275
Holy Water Font, Worship Hum 164	*	$68-$300
Home From Market Hum 198	*	$375-$800
Home From Market Hum 198/2/0	*	$190-$375

Due to space constraints, a range of pricing has been provided in some instances. Please consult the 12th edition of Luckey's Hummel® Figurines & Plates Identification and Price Guide *for individual pricing based upon trademark variations.*

Hum No. 170/I *School Boys*, $1480-$1900

Hum No. 174 *She Loves Me,*
She Loves Me Not!, $240-$700

Hum No. 175 *Mother's Darling*, $250-$800

	Year	Price
M.I. Hummel		
Home From Market Hum 198/I	*	$240-$500
Homeward Bound Hum 334	*	$400-$5000
Honey Lover Hum 312	1955	$235-$6000
Horse Trainer Hum 423	1990	$268-$280
Hosanna Hum 480	1989	$140
Hum 148	1941	N/A
Hum 149	1941	N/A
Hum 236 A&B	1954	$10,000-$15,000
Hum 156	1943	N/A
I'll Protect Him Hum 483	1989	$115
I'm Carefree Hum 633	1994	$440-$1000
I'm Here Hum 478	1989	$145
In D Major Hum 430	1989	$255
In The Meadow Hum 459	1987	$255
In Tune Hum 414	1981	$310-$4000
Is It Raining? Hum 420	1989	$350
Jesus Standing With Lamb In Arms, Hum 215	1951	N/A
Joyful & Let's Sing Wd Bookends, Hum 120	*	$10,000-20,000
Joyful Hum 53	*	$140-$450
Joyful Noise Hum 643/0	1999	$130-$200
Joyful Noise Mini Figurine Hum 643/4/0	1999	$130
Joyful, Box (New Style) Hum III/53	*	$300-$350

Hum No. 176/0 *Happy Birthday*, $280-$500

Hum No. 177 *School Girls*, $1480-$5000

Hum No. 178 *Photographer*, $335-$1100

	Year	Price
M.I. Hummel		
Joyful, Box (Old Style)		
Hum III/53	*	**$475-$550**
Joyous News Hum 27/3	*	**$280-$2000**
Joyous News Hum 27/I	*	**$250-$500**
Joyous News Hum 27/III	*	**$253**
Jubilee Hum 416	1985	**$500-$600**
Just Dozing Hum 451	1984	**$265**
Just Dozing Hum 451	1995	**$262-$270**
Just Fishing Hum 373	1985	**$250-$1500**
Just Resting Hum 112	*	**$700-$850**
Just Resting Hum 112/3/0	*	**$185-$550**
Just Resting Hum 112/I	*	**$320-$800**
Just Resting, Table		
Lamp Hum II/112	*	**$375-$800**
Just Resting, Table		
Lamp Hum 225	*	**$500-$800**
Just Resting, Table		
Lamp Hum 225/I	*	**$350-$600**

Due to space constraints, a range of pricing has been provided in some instances. Please consult the 12th edition of Luckey's Hummel® Figurines & Plates Identification and Price Guide *for individual pricing based upon trademark variations.*

Hum No. 183 *Forest Shrine*, $595-$1900

Hum No. 186 *Sweet Music*, $250-$750

Hum No. 187 *Retailer Plaque, U.S.A.*, $175-$1500

Hum No. 194 *Watchful Angel*, $385-$2100

Hum No. 195/2/0 *Barnyard Hero*, $205-$450

	Year	Price
M.I. Hummel		
Just Resting, Table Lamp Hum 225/II	*	$400-$800
Kid's Club Collector's Set Hum 699, 771, 698	2002	$650
Kindergartner Hum 467	1987	$255
Kiss Me Hum 311	*	$335-$550
Kitty Kisses Hum 2033	2002	$195
Knit One, Purl One Hum 432	1983	$160
Knitting Lesson Hum 256	*	$535-$1150
Land In Sight Hum 530	1991	$1800-$2250
Latest News Hum 184	*	$360-$1100
Let's Play Hum 2051/B	1999	$95
Let's Sing Hum 110	*	$325-$600
Let's Sing Hum 110/I	*	$195-$375
Let's Sing Hum 110/0	*	$160-$500
Let's Sing, Ashtray Hum 114	*	$150-$1000
Let's Sing, Box (New Style) Hum III/110	*	$300-$350
Let's Sing, Box (Old Style) Hum III/110	*	$475-$550
Letter To Santa Claus Prototype Hum 340	1956	$15,000-20,000
Letter To Santa Hum 340	*	$400-$1000
Light The Way	2000	$180
Light The Way Mini	2000	$120

Hum No. 196 *Telling Her Secret*, $800-$1500

	Year	Price
M.I. Hummel		
Little Architect Hum 410/I	1993	$370
Little Architect, The Hum 410	1978	$3000-$4000
Little Band (On Base) Hum 392	✿	$275-$450
Little Band On Music Box	✿	$400-$500
Little Band, Candleholder/Box Hum 388	✿	$275-$500
Little Bookkeeper Hum 306	✿	$335-$1500
Little Cellist Hum 89	✿	$1250-$1600
Little Cellist Hum 89/I	✿	$270-$850
Little Cellist Hum 89/II	✿	$450-$1500
Little Drummer Hum 240	✿	$185-$400
Little Fiddler Hum 2/4/0	✿	$130-$140
Little Fiddler Hum 2/I	✿	$415-$1500
Little Fiddler Hum 2/II	✿	$1110-$3500
Little Fiddler Hum 2/III	✿	$1205-$4000
Little Fiddler Hum 2/0	✿	$325-$850
Little Fiddler Hum 4	✿	$240-$800

Due to space constraints, a range of pricing has been provided in some instances. Please consult the 12th edition of Luckey's Hummel® Figurines & Plates Identification and Price Guide *for individual pricing based upon trademark variations.*

Hum No. 197 *Be Patient*, $250-$1000

Hum No. 198/2/0 *Home From Market*, $190-$375

Hum No. 199 *Feeding Time*, $250-$1000

	Year	Price

M.I. Hummel

	Year	Price
Little Fiddler, Plaque (Rare) Hum 93	*	**$3000-$4000**
Little Fiddler, Plaque Hum 93	*	**$150-$575**
Little Fiddler, Plaque Wood Frame, Hum 107	*	**$3000-$4000**
Little Gabriel Hum 32/I	*	**$1200-$2500**
Little Gabriel Hum 32/0	*	**$180-$550**
Little Gabriel, 5 In. Hum 32	*	**$165-$200**
Little Gabriel, Hum 32	1935	**$2000-$2500**
Little Gardener Hum 74	*	**$150-$550**
Little Goat Herder Hum 200	*	**$500-$850**
Little Goat Herder Hum 200/I	*	**$270-$550**
Little Goat Herder Hum 200/0	*	**$250-$500**
Little Goat Herder, Bookends Hum 250 A&B	*	**$300-$750**
Little Guardian Hum 145	*	**$175-$550**
Little Helper Hum 73	*	**$150-$500**
Little Hiker Hum 16	*	**$450-$750**
Little Hiker Hum 16/2/0	*	**$140-$450**
Little Hiker Hum 16/I	*	**$245-$700**
Little Nurse Hum 376	1982	**$295-$3000**
Little Pharmacist Hum 322	*	**$280-$5000**
Little Scholar Hum 80	*	**$270-$800**
Little Scholar Hum 80/2/0	2002	**$175**
Little Shopper Hum 96	*	**$180-$550**
Little Sweeper Hum 171	*	**$185-$500**

Hum No. 201 *Retreat To Safety*, $200-$1200

Hum No. 203/I *Signs Of Spring*, $275-$600

Hum No. 214C *Angel, Good Night*, $115-$200 (color) or $265-$415 (white)

Hum No. 214/D/I *Angel Serenade*, $115-$200 (color) or $165-$290 (white)

Hum No. 214O *Lamb*, $30-$130

	Year	Price
M.I. Hummel		
Little Sweeper Hum 171/4/0	*	**$130**
Little Sweeper Hum 171/0	*	**$185**
Little Tailor Hum 308	*	**$305-$350**
Little Thrifty, Bank Hum 118	*	**$185-$650**
Little Troubador Hum 558	1999	**$145**
Little Velma Hum 219	1952	**$4000-$6000**
Little Visitor Hum 563	1994	**$200-$225**
Lost Sheep Hum 68	*	**$350-$750**
Lost Sheep Hum 68/2/0	*	**$160-$350**
Lost Sheep Hum 68/0	*	**$200-$450**
Lost Stocking Hum 374	*	**$185-$1500**
Love From Above Hum 481	1989	**$125-$150**
Lucky Boy Hum 335	1995	**$220-$250**
Lucky Fellow Hum 560	1992	**$110**
Lullaby, Candleholder Hum 24/I	*	**$215-$700**
Lullaby, Candleholder Hum 24/III	*	**$475-$1900**

Due to space constraints, a range of pricing has been provided in some instances. Please consult the 12th edition of Luckey's Hummel® Figurines & Plates Identification and Price Guide *for individual pricing based upon trademark variations.*

Hum No. 218/2/0 *Birthday Serenade*, $210-$700

	Year	Price

M.I. Hummel

	Year	Price
M.I. Hummel (English), Plaque Hum 187 A	*	$110-$225
Madonna Holding Child Hum 151	1955	$9000-$12,000
Madonna Holding Child Hum 155	1943	N/A
Mail Is Here, The-Plaque Hum 140	*	$250-$950
Mail Is Here, The Hum 226	*	$655-$1350
Mail Is Here, The Plaq. Overglaze Hum 140	*	$1000-$1500
Make A Wish Hum 475	1989	$240
Making New Friends	2000	$630
March Winds Hum 43	*	$180-$600
Max And Moritz Hum 123	*	$270-$800
Meditation, Hum 13	*	$4000-$5000
Meditation Hum 13/2/0	*	$160-$350
Meditation Hum 13/II	*	$350-$5000
Meditation Hum 13/O	*	$245-$850
Meditation Hum 13/V	*	$1200-$5000
Merry Christmas, Plaque Hum 323	1979	$140-$3000
Merry Wanderer Hum 7/I	*	$425-$1750
Merry Wanderer Hum 7/II	*	$1200-$3500
Merry Wanderer Hum 7/III	*	$1250-$4000
Merry Wanderer Hum 7/0	*	$330-$1000

Hum No. 220 *We Congratulate*, $200-$575

Hum No. 226 *The Mail Is Here*, $655-$1350

Hum No. 239C *Boy With Horse*, $73-$200

	Year	Price
M.I. Hummel		
Merry Wanderer Hum 7/X	*	**$15,000-$25,000**
Merry Wanderer Hum 11	*	**$600-$750**
Merry Wanderer Hum 11/2/0	*	**$170-$550**
Merry Wanderer Hum 11/0	*	**$225-$700**
Merry Wanderer, Plaque Hum 92	*	**$150-$575**
Merry Wanderer/Plaq. Wd Frame, Hum 106	*	**$3000-$4000**
Message Of Love Hum 2050/A	1999	**$95**
Mischief Maker Hum 342	*	**$320-$1000**
Morning Stroll Hum 375	1964	**$3000-$4000**
Morning Stroll Hum 375/3/0	1994	**$215**
Mother's Darling Hum 175	*	**$250-$800**
Mother's Helper Hum 133	*	**$258-$800**
Mountaineer Hum 315	*	**$250-$1000**
My Best Friend Hum 2049/B	1999	**$95**
My Wish Is Small Hum 463/0	1992	**$250-$2500**

Due to space constraints, a range of pricing has been provided in some instances. Please consult the 12th edition of Luckey's Hummel® Figurines & Plates Identification and Price Guide *for individual pricing based upon trademark variations.*

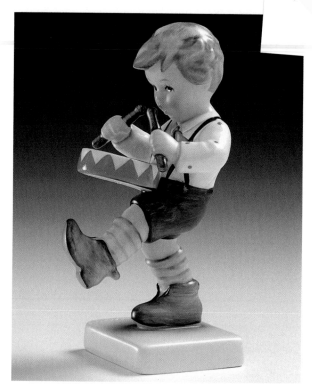

Hum No. 240 *Little Drummer*, $185-$400

Hum No. 256 *Knitting Lesson*, $535-$1150

Hum No. 257/0 *For Mother*, $255

Hum No. 261 *Angel Duet*, $270-$850

Hum No. 264
Heavenly Angel,
$500-$750

Hum No. 269
Apple Tree Girl,
$50-$75

	Year	**Price**
M.I. Hummel		
Nap, A Hum 534	1991	**$155**
Nimble Fingers Hum 758	1996	**$255**
Not For You! Hum 317	*	**$300-$1000**
Nutcracker Sweet Collector's Set Hum 2130	2002	**$375**
Old Man Reading Newspaper Hum 181	1948	**$15,000-$20,000**
Old Man Reading Newspaper/ Tbl Lamp Hum 202	1948	**$15,000-$20,000**
Old Man Walking To Market Hum 191	1948	**$15,000-$20,000**
Old Woman Knitting Hum 189	1948	**$15,000-$20,000**
Old Woman Walking To Market Hum 190	1948	**$15,000-$20,000**
On Holiday "Holiday Shopper" Hum 350	1981	**$180-$5000**
On Holiday Hum 350	1981	**$200-$2000**
On Secret Path Hum 386	*	**$300-$1500**

Due to space constraints, a range of pricing has been provided in some instances. Please consult the 12th edition of Luckey's Hummel® Figurines & Plates Identification and Price Guide *for individual pricing based upon trademark variations.*

Hum No. 275
Umbrella Girl,
$125-$150

Hum No. 276
Postman,
$200-$250

Hum No. 278
Chick Girl,
$50-$75

Hum No. 279
Playmates,
$200-$250

Hum No. 280
Stormy Weather,
$100-$150

Hum No. 282
Auf Wiedersehen,
$150-$200

	Year	Price

M.I. Hummel

	Year	Price
Once Upon A Time Hum 2051/A	1999	**$95**
One For You, One For Me Hum 482	1989	**$140**
One Plus One Hum 556	1993	**$165-$200**
Ooh, My Tooth Hum 533	1995	**$145**
Orchestra Hum 212	1951	**N/A**
Out Of Danger Hum 56 B	*	**$345-$650**
Out Of Danger, Table Lamp, Hum 44 B	*	**$325-$650**
Parade Of Lights Hum 616	1993	**$305**
Pay Attention Hum 426/3/0	1999	**$190-$2000**
Peaceful Blessing Hum 814	1999	**$195**
Pen Pals	1996	**$55**
Photographer Hum 178	*	**$335-$1100**
Pixie Hum 768	1995	**$145**
Playmates Hum 58	*	**$500-$1050**
Playmates Hum 58/2/0	*	**$185-$200**
Playmates Hum 58/I	*	**$320-$1000**
Playmates Hum 58/0	*	**$205-$700**
Playmates, Box (New Style) Hum III/58	*	**$300-$350**
Playmates, Box (Old Style) Hum III/58	*	**$425-$550**

Hum No. 283
Feeding Time,
$250-$300

**Hum No.
288 *Wayside
Harmony,*
$150-$200**

Hum No. 290 *Doctor*, $150-$200

Hum No. 293 *For Father*, $100-$150

	Year	Price
M.I. Hummel		
Playmates/Chick Girl		
Bookends Hum 61 A&B	*	$400-$1250
Poet, The Hum 397	1974	$3000-$4000
Poet, The Hum 397/I	1994	$260-$285
Postman Hum 119	1989	$255-$750
Postman Hum 119/2/0	*	$185
Postman Hum 119/0	*	$250
Prayer Before Battle Hum 20	*	$195-$650
Prayer Before Battle,		
Ashtray Hum 19	*	$5000-$10,000
Pretzel Boy Collector's Set	2000	$185
Professor, The Hum 320	1955	$4000-$5000
Professor, The Hum 320/0	*	$245-$258
Puppy Love & Serenade/		
Dog Bkends Hum 122	*	$10,000-$20,000
Puppy Love Hum 1	*	$305-$1000
Puppy Pause Hum 2032	2002	$195
Quartet, Plaque Hum 134	*	$250-$1000
Retreat To Safety Hum 201	*	$650-$1200

Due to space constraints, a range of pricing has been provided in some instances. Please consult the 12th edition of Luckey's Hummel® Figurines & Plates Identification and Price Guide *for individual pricing based upon trademark variations.*

Hum No. 294 *Sweet Greetings*, $100-$150

Hum No. 295 *Surprise Plate*, $100-$150

Hum No. 299 *Autumn Glory*, **$200**

	Year	Price

M.I. Hummel

	Year	Price
Retreat To Safety Hum 201/2/0	*	**$200-$450**
Retreat To Safety Hum 201/I	*	**$360-$700**
Retreat To Safety, Plaque Hum 126	*	**$185-$700**
Ride Into Christmas Hum 396	*	**$525-$2500**
Ride Into Christmas Hum 396/2/0	*	**$290-$325**
Ride Into Christmas Hum 396/I	*	**$540**
Ring Around The Rosie Hum 348	1957	**$3200-$5000**
Ring Around The Rosie Musical Hum 348	1995	**$3200-$12,000**
Run-A-Way Hum 327	*	**$310-$325**
Saint George Hum 55	*	**$350-$3000**
Scamp Hum 553	1991	**$135**
School Boy Hum 82	*	**$625-$775**
School Boy Hum 82/2/0	*	**$170-$600**
School Boy Hum 82/II	*	**$500-$1600**
School Boy Hum 82/0	*	**$235-$775**
School Boys Hum 170	*	**$2200-$5000**
School Boys Hum 170/I	*	**$1480-$1900**
School Boys Hum 170/III	*	**$2750-$3100**
School Girl Hum 81	*	**$350-$750**

Hum No. 300 *Bird Watcher*, $270-$5000

	Year	Price
M.I. Hummel		
School Girl Hum 81/2/0	*	$180-$600
School Girl Hum 81/0	*	$225-$700
School Girls Hum 177	*	$3200-$5000
School Girls Hum 177/I	*	$1480-$1900
School Girls Hum 177/III	*	$2750-$3100
Searching Angel,		
Plaque Hum 310	1979	$135-$2000
Sensitive Hunter Hum 6	*	$850-$1000
Sensitive Hunter Hum 6/2/0	*	$170-$180
Sensitive Hunter Hum 6/I	*	$300-$1000
Sensitive Hunter Hum 6/II	*	$350-$2000
Sensitive Hunter Hum 6/0	*	$250-$800
Seraphim Soprano		
Hum 2096/R	2002	$135
Serenade Hum 85	*	$775-$1550
Serenade Hum 85/4/0	*	$130
Serenade Hum 85/II	*	$500-$1500
Serenade Hum 85/0	*	$160-$500

Due to space constraints, a range of pricing has been provided in some instances. Please consult the 12th edition of Luckey's Hummel® Figurines & Plates Identification and Price Guide *for individual pricing based upon trademark variations.*

Hum No. 305 *Builder*, $305-$5000

Hum No. 307 *Good Hunting*, $300-$5000

Hum No. 308 *Little Tailor*, $305-$350

Hum No. 311 *Kiss Me*, $335-$550

Hum No. 312 *Honey Lover*, $235-$6000

	Year	Price
M.I. Hummel		
She Loves Me, Candleholder Hum 678	1990	$200-$250
She Loves Me, She Loves Me Not! Hum 174	*	$240-$700
She Loves Me...Not, Table Lamp Hum 227	*	$375-$850
Shepherd Boy Hum 395	1996	$280-$315
Shepherd's Boy Hum 64	*	$330-$900
Shining Light Hum 358	*	$110-$150
Shrine, Table Lamp Hum 100	*	$8000-$10,000
Signs Of Spring Hum 203	*	$550-$1000
Signs Of Spring Hum 203/2/0	*	$225-$1500
Signs Of Spring Hum 203/I	*	$275-$600
Signs Of Spring With Two Shoes Hum 203/2/0	*	$115-$1500
Silent Night Candleholdr/ Blk Child Hum 54	*	$7500-$12,000
Silent Night Candleholder Hum 54	*	$365
Silent Night/Blk Child/ Advent Grp Hum 31	*	$20,000-$25,000
Silent Night/Wht Child/ Advent Grp Hum 31	*	$10,000-$15,000
Sing Along Hum 433	1987	$330
Sing With Me Hum 405	1985	$360-$4000

Hum No. 315 *Mountaineer*, $250-$1000

Hum No. 317 *Not for You*, $300-$1000

Hum No. 318 *Art Critic*, $315-$5000

	Year	Price

M.I. Hummel

	Year	Price
Singing Lesson (Without Base) Hum 41	❈	$5000-$10,000
Singing Lesson Hum 63	❈	$155-$550
Singing Lesson, Ashtray Hum 34	❈	$175-$650
Singing Lesson, Box (New Style) Hum III/63	❈	$300-$350
Singing Lesson, Box (Old Style) Hum III/63	❈	$475-$550
Sister Hum 98	❈	$325-$700
Sister Hum 98/2/0	❈	$180-$250
Sister Hum 98/0	❈	$230-$325
Skier Hum 59	❈	$250-$900
Sleep Tight Hum 424	1990	$265-$280
Smart Little Sister Hum 346	❈	$300-$5000
Soldier Boy Hum 332	❈	$250-$5000
Soloist Hum 135	❈	$180-$550
Soloist Hum 135/4/0	❈	$135
Soloist Hum 135/0	❈	$175

Due to space constraints, a range of pricing has been provided in some instances. Please consult the 12th edition of Luckey's Hummel® Figurines & Plates Identification and Price Guide *for individual pricing based upon trademark variations.*

Hum No. 319 *Doll Bath*, $355-$5000

Hum No. 320/0 *The Professor*, $245-$258

Hum No. 321/I *Wash Day*, $355-$365

	Year	Price
M.I. Hummel		
Song Of Praise Hum 454	1988	**$140**
Sound The Trumpet		
Hum 457	1988	**$140**
Sounds Of The Mandolin		
Hum 438	1988	**$165**
Spring Cheer Hum 72	*	**$200-$650**
Spring Dance Hum 353/I	*	**$550-$2000**
Spring Dance Hum 353/0	*	**$395-$5000**
Standing Boy, Plaque		
Hum 168	*	**$200-$1100**
Standing Madonna With		
Child Hum 247	1955	**$10,000-$15,000**
Star Gazer Hum 132	*	**$258-$800**
Stitch In Time Hum 255	*	**$325-$800**
Stitch In Time Hum 255/4/0	*	**$115-$140**
Stormy Weather Hum 71	*	**$560-$1350**
Stormy Weather Hum 71/2/0	*	**$365-$380**
Stormy Weather Hum 71/I	*	**$550**
Storybook Time Hum 458	1991	**$495**
Street Singer Hum 131	*	**$245-$700**
String Symphony		
Hum 2096/D	2002	**$135**
Strolling Along Hum 5	*	**$275-$950**
Strum Along Hum 557	1999	**$155**
Supreme Protection		
Hum 364	*	**$3000-$4000**

Hum No. 322 *Little Pharmacist*, $280-$5000

Hum No. 328 *Carnival*, $250-$5000

Hum No. 333 *Blessed Event*, $400-$5000

	Year	Price

M.I. Hummel

	Year	Price
Supreme Protection Hum 364 (Altered J)	*	$600-$850
Surprise Hum 94	*	$550-$1000
Surprise Hum 94/3/0	*	$190-$550
Surprise Hum 94/I	*	$325-$950
Swaying Lullaby Collector's Set	2000	$325
Swaying Lullaby, Plaque Hum 165	*	$200-$1100
Sweet As Can Be Birthday Sampler Hum 541	1999	$170
Sweet Greetings Hum 352	1981	$215-$5000
Sweet Music Hum 186	*	$250-$750
Sweet Music With Striped Slippers Hum 186	*	$1000-$1500
Sweet Offering Hum 549	1992	$100-$125
Teacher's Pet Hum 2125	2002	$175
Telling Her Secret Hum 196	*	$800-$1500
Telling Her Secret Hum 196/I	*	$400-$950

Due to space constraints, a range of pricing has been provided in some instances. Please consult the 12th edition of Luckey's Hummel® Figurines & Plates Identification and Price Guide *for individual pricing based upon trademark variations.*

Hum No. 334 *Homeward Bound*, $400-$5000

Hum No. 337 *Cinderella*, $355-$5000

Hum No. 340 *Letter To Santa*, $400-$1000

Hum No. 342 *Mischief Maker*, $320-$1000

Hum No. 345 *A Fair Measure*, $350-$5000

	Year	Price
M.I. Hummel		
Telling Her Secret Hum 196/0	*	$375-$750
Thoughtful Hum 415	1981	$270-$4000
Timid Little Sister Hum 394	1981	$530-$4000
Tiny Baby In Crib,		
Wall Plaq., Hum 138	*	$2000-$5000
To Keep You Warm Hum 759	1995	$258-$265
To Market Hum 49	*	$600-$1700
To Market Hum 49/3/0	*	$195-$650
To Market Hum 49/I	*	$450-$1700
To Market Hum 49/0	*	$325-$1000
To Market, Table Lamp		
Hum 101	*	$500-$1000
To Market, Table Lamp		
Hum 223	*	$495-$850
To Market,Table Lamp		
(Pl. Post) Hum 101	*	$6,000-$10,000
To Market,Tbl Lamp		
Tree Trk Post Hum 101	*	$1500-$2000
Trumpet Boy Hum 97	*	$150-$525
Tuba Player Hum 437	1989	$345
Tuneful Angel Hum 359	*	$110-$150
Tuneful Good Night,		
Plaque Hum 180	*	$200-$800
Tuneful Trio Hum 757	1996	$475-$500
Umbrella Boy Hum		
152/A/2/0	2002	$300

Hum No. 347 *Adventure Bound*, $4350-$15,000

	Year	Price
M.I. Hummel		
Umbrella Boy Hum 152	*	$2400-$7000
Umbrella Boy Hum 152 A	*	$1825-$2800
Umbrella Boy Hum 152/II A	*	$1750-$1900
Umbrella Boy Hum 152/0 A	*	$715-$1600
Umbrella Girl Hum 152/B/2/0	2002	$300
Umbrella Girl Hum 152 B	*	$1825-$7000
Umbrella Girl Hum 152/II B	*	$1750-$1900
Umbrella Girl Hum 152/0 B	*	$715-$1600
Vacation Time, Plaque Hum 125	*	$225-$750
Village Boy Hum 51	*	$900-$1150
Village Boy Hum 51/2/0	*	$185-$550
Village Boy Hum 51/3/0	*	$150-$450
Village Boy Hum 51/I	*	$300-$1100
Village Boy Hum 51/0	*	$280-$900
Visiting An Invalid Hum 382	*	$250-$1500
Volunteer Table Lamp, Hum 102	*	$8000-$10,000
Volunteers Hum 50	*	$1250-$1500
Volunteers Hum 50/2/0	*	$265-$500
Volunteers Hum 50/I	*	$450-$1500
Volunteers Hum 50/0	*	$375-$1100
Waiter Hum 154	*	$550-$1150
Waiter Hum 154/I	*	$325-$1000
Waiter Hum 154/O	*	$270-$800
Waiter With Whisky Hum 154/0	*	$1600-$2100

Hum No. 348 *Ring Around The Rosie*, $3200-$5000

	Year	Price
M.I. Hummel		
Wash Day Hum 321	*	$275-$1000
Wash Day Hum 321	1989	$360
Wash Day Hum 321/I		$355-$365
Wash Day Hum 321/4/0	*	$125-$140
Watchful Angel Hum 194	*	$385-$2100
Wayside Devotion Hum 28	*	$1700-$1900
Wayside Devotion Hum 28/II	*	$510-$1500
Wayside Devotion Hum 28/III	*	$600-$1700
Wayside Harmony Hum 111	*	$700-$850
Wayside Harmony Hum 111/3/0	*	$185-$550
Wayside Harmony Hum 111/I	*	$320
Wayside Harmony, Table Lamp Hum II/111	*	$375-$800
Wayside Harmony, Table Lamp Hum 224	*	$500-$800
Wayside Harmony, Table Lamp Hum 224/I	*	$350-$600
Wayside Harmony, Table Lamp Hum 224/II	*	$400-$800
We Congratulate (With Base) Hum 220	1952	$200-$400
We Congratulate (With Base) Hum 220/2/0	1952	$475-$575
We Wish You The Best Hum 600	1991	$1700-$2100

Hum No. 350 *On Holiday*, $200-$2000

Hum No. 353/0 *Spring Dance*, $395-$5000

Hum No. 355 *Autumn Harvest*, $250-$3000

Hum No. 363 *Big House Cleaning*, $335-$5000

Hum No. 364 *Supreme Protection*, $3000-$4000

	Year	Price

M.I. Hummel

	Year	Price
Weary Wanderer Hum 204	*	$280-$900
What's New? Hum 418	1990	$350-$380
Where Are You? Hum427/3/0	1999	$190-$2000
Which Hand? Hum 258	*	$235-$825
Whistler's Duet Hum 413	1991	$330-$4000
Whitsuntide Hum 163	*	$330-$1200
Winter Song Hum 476	1988	$150
With Loving Greetings Hum 309	1983	$220-$5000
Wonder Of Christmas Hum 2015 With Steiff Bear	1999	$575
Worship Hum 84	*	$475-$1500
Worship Hum 84/0	*	$200-$600
Worship Hum 84/V	*	$1125-$3000

M.I. Hummel Century Collection

	Year	Price
Call To Worship, Clock Hum 441	1988	$1400-$1500

Due to space constraints, a range of pricing has been provided in some instances. Please consult the 12th edition of Luckey's Hummel® Figurines & Plates Identification and Price Guide *for individual pricing based upon trademark variations.*

Hum No. 367 *Busy Student*, $200-$1100

Hum No. 369 *Follow The Leader*, $1390-$5000

Hum No. 371 *Daddy's Girls*, $275-$4000

	Year	Price

M.I. Hummel Century Collection

	Year	Price
Chapel Time, Clock Hum 442	1986	$2500-$3000
Echoes Of Joy Hum 642/0	1998	$200
Echoes Of Joy Miniature Hum 642/4/0	1998	$130
Harmony In Four Parts Hum 471	1989	$2000-$2500
Heart's Delight Hum 698	1998	$230
Here's My Heart Hum 766	1998	$1500-$1600
Let's Tell The World Hum 487	1990	$1500-$1800
Love In Bloom Hum 699	1998	$245
On Our Way Hum 472	1992	$1200-$3000
Rock-A-Bye Hum 574	1994	$1400-$1600
Roses Are Red Hum 762	1998	$135
Strike Up The Band Hum 668	1995	$1400-$1600
Summertime Enterprise Hum 428/3/0	1998	$160
Welcome Spring Hum 635	1993	$1600-$1800

M.I. Hummel Collector's Choice

	Year	Price
True Friendship Hum 402	2002	$365-$4000

M.I. Hummel Collectors Club Anniversary

	Year	Price
Camera Ready Hum 2132	2002	$525
Flower Girl Hum 548	1990	$150-$225
Honey Lover Hum 312/I	1991	$235-$500
Little Pair, The- Hum 449	1990	$225-$400

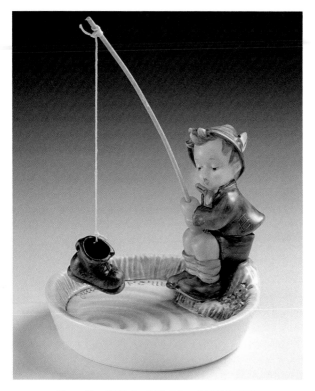

Hum No. 373 *Just Fishing*, $250-$1500

Hum No. 374 *Lost Stocking*, **$185-$1500**

Hum No. 375/3/0 *Morning Stroll*, $215

	Year	Price

M.I. Hummel Collectors Club Exclusives

Item	Year	Price
At Grandpa's Hum 621	1994	$1500-$1600
Birthday Candle, Candleholder Hum 440	1986	$350-$400
Cheeky Fellow Hum 554	1992	$150
Coffee Break Hum 409	1984	$300-$4000
Daisies Don't Tell Hum 380	1981	$275-$4000
For Keeps Hum 630	1994	$100-$125
Gift From A Friend Hum 485	1991	$250-$350
Hello World Hum 429	1989	$300-$400
I Brought You A Gift Hum 479	1989	$125-$175
I Didn't Do It Hum 626	1993	$200-$225
I Wonder Hum 486	1990	$250-$350
It's Cold Hum 421	1982	$350-$400
Little Troubadour Hum 558	1994	$145
Morning Concert Hum 447	1987	$250-$300
My Wish Is Small Hum 463	1992	$250-$2500
Smiling Through Hum 408	1985	$4000-$5000
Smiling Through, Plaque Hum 690	1978	$50-$75

Due to space constraints, a range of pricing has been provided in some instances. Please consult the 12th edition of Luckey's Hummel® Figurines & Plates Identification and Price Guide for individual pricing based upon trademark variations.

Hum No. 377 *Bashful*, $250-$4000

Hum No. 378 *Easter Greetings*, $225-$4000

Hum No. 381 *Flower Vendor*, $305-$4000

	Year	Price

M.I. Hummel Collectors Club Exclusives

	Year	Price
Story From Grandma Hum 620	1995	**$1500-$1600**
Surprise, The- Hum 431	1988	**$300-$3000**
Sweet As Can Be Hum 541	1993	**$170**
Two Hands, One Treat		
Hum 493	1991	**$125-$150**
Valentine Gift Hum 387	1977	**$450-$7000**
Valentine Joy Hum 399	1980	**$250-$7500**
What Now? Hum 422	1983	**$350-$400**

M.I. Hummel Collectors Club Exclusives

Bust Of Sister M.I.		
Hummel H-3	1979	**$350-$400**

M.I. Hummel Just For You

Proud Moments	2000	**$320**

M.I. Hummel Madonna

Flower Madonna,		
Color Hum 10/I	*	**$475-$950**
Flower Madonna,		
White Hum 10/I	*	**$230-$600**
Flower Madonna,		
Color Hum 10/III	*	**$500-$900**
Flower Madonna,		
White Hum 10/III	*	**$300-$750**
Madonna Holding		
Child, Blue Hum 151	1977	**$900-$3000**

Hum No. 383 *Going Home*, $395-$4000

Hum No. 384 *Easter Time*, $300-$1500

Hum No. 385/4/0 *Chicken-Licken*, $115-$140

	Year	Price
M.I. Hummel Madonna		
Madonna Holding Child, White Hum 151	1977	$400-$2500
Madonna Plaque Hum 48	*	$650-$850
Madonna Plaque Hum 48/II	*	$130-$800
Madonna Plaque Hum 48/0	*	$85-$375
Madonna Plaque Hum 48/V	*	$1000-$2000
Madonna With Halo, Color Hum 45/I	*	$160-$400
Madonna With Halo, White Hum 45/I	*	$75-$200
Madonna With Halo White Hum 45/III	*	$105-$350
Madonna With Halo, Color Hum 45/III	*	$150-$600
Madonna With Halo, Color Hum 45/0	*	$60-$275
Madonna With Halo, White Hum 45/0 white	*	$40-$175

Due to space constraints, a range of pricing has been provided in some instances. Please consult the 12th edition of Luckey's Hummel® Figurines & Plates Identification and Price Guide *for individual pricing based upon trademark variations.*

Hum No. 386 *On Secret Path*, **$300-$1500**

Hum No. 389 *Girl With Sheet Of Music*, $110-$275

Hum No. 390 *Boy With Accordion*, $110-$275

	Year	**Price**

M.I. Hummel Madonna

Madonna Without Halo, Color Hum 46/I	*	$140-$400
Madonna Without Halo, White Hum 46/I	*	$85-$250
Madonna Without Halo, Color Hum 46/III	*	$150-$600
Madonna Without Halo, White Hum 46/III	*	$105-$350
Madonna Without Halo, Color Hum 46/0	*	$60-$275
Madonna Without Halo, White Hum 46/0	*	$40-$175

M.I. Hummel Moments In Time

Soap Box Derby Hum 2121	2002	$1250

M.I. Hummel Nativity

Angel Kneeling/Serenade, Color Hum 214D	*	$115-$200
Angel Kneeling/Serenade, White Hum 214D	*	$165-$290
Angel Serenade (Large) Hum 260E	*	$155-$170
Angel/Good Night, Color Hum 214C	*	$115-$200
Angel, Good Night, White Hum 214C	*	$265-$415

Hum No. 394 *Timid Little Sister*, $530-$4000

Hum No. 397/I *The Poet*, $260-$285

Hum No. 405 *Sing With Me*, $360-$4000

	Year	Price
M.I. Hummel Nativity		
Cow, Lying (Large)		
Hum 260M	*	**$170-$190**
Donkey, Color Hum 214J	*	**$95-$160**
Donkey, White Hum 214J	*	**$130-$255**
Donkey Hum 214J/0	1989	**$63-$75**
Donkey, Standing		
(Large) Hum 260L	*	**$155-$170**
Good Night (Large) Hum 260D	*	**$160-$180**
Infant Jesus (Large)		
Hum 260C	*	**$130-$150**
Infant Jesus, Color		
Hum 214A/K	*	**$85**
Infant Jesus Hum,		
White 214A/K	*	**$60-$70**
Infant Jesus Hum 214A/K/1	*	**$80**
Infant Jesus Hum 214A/K/0	1988	**$64**
Joseph, Color Hum 214B	*	**$215-$400**
Joseph, White Hum 214B	*	**$145**
Joseph Hum 214B/0	1988	**$170**

Due to space constraints, a range of pricing has been provided in some instances. Please consult the 12th edition of Luckey's Hummel® Figurines & Plates Identification and Price Guide for individual pricing based upon trademark variations.

Hum No. 408 *Smiling Through*, $4000-$5000

Hum No. 410/I *The Little Architect*, $370

Hum No. 412 *Bath Time*, $535-$4000

	Year	Price

M.I. Hummel Nativity

	Year	Price
King On One Knee Hum 214M/0	*	**$175**
King On One Knee, Color Hum 214M	*	**$215-$415**
King On One Knee, White Hum 214M	*	**$225-$475**
King On Two Knees Hum 214N/0	*	**$175**
King Standing Hum 214l/0	1990	**$190**
King, Knee With Cash Box, Color Hum 214N	*	**$200-$385**
King, Knee With Cash Box, White Hum 214N	*	**$225-$475**
King, Kneeling (Large) Hum 260P	*	**$540-$570**
King, Standing (Large) Hum 260O	*	**$565-$615**
Lamb Hum 214O	*	**$55-$130**
Lamb, Color Hum 214O	*	**$30-$55**
Lamb Hum 214O/0	1989	**$30**
Little Tooter (Large) Hum 260K	*	**$195-$220**
Little Tooter Hum 214H/0	1991	**$127**
Madonna (Large) Hum 260A	*	**$575-$650**
Mary Hum 214/A/M/0	1988	**$170**

Hum No. 414 *In Tune*, $310-$4000

Hum No. 416 *Jubilee*, $500-$600

Hum No. 418 *What's New?*, $350-$380

	Year	Price

M.I. Hummel Nativity

	Year	Price
Moorish King, Standing (Large) Hum 260N	*	**$565-$615**
Moorish King, Standing, Color Hum 214l	*	**$220-$415**
Moorish King, Standing, White Hum 214l	*	**$225-$475**
Nativity Set (Large) 16 Pieces Hum 260	*	**$5745-$6305**
One Sheep, Lying (Large) Hum 260R	*	**$65-$80**
Ox (Cow), Color Hum 214K	*	**$95-$160**
Ox (Cow), White Hum 214K	*	**$130-$255**
Ox Hum 214K/0	1989	**$64**
Saint Joseph (Large) Hum 260B	*	**$575-$650**
Sheep, Standing With Lamb (Large) Hum 260H	*	**$110-$125**
Shepherd Boy With Flute, Color Hum 214H	*	**$160-$280**

Due to space constraints, a range of pricing has been provided in some instances. Please consult the 12th edition of Luckey's Hummel® Figurines & Plates Identification and Price Guide *for individual pricing based upon trademark variations.*

Hum No. 420 *Is It Raining?*, $350

Hum No. 421 *It's Cold*, $350-$400

Hum No. 423 *Horse Trainer*, $268-$280

	Year	Price

M.I. Hummel Nativity

	Year	Price
Shepherd Boy With Flute, White Hum 214H	*	$170-$320
Shepherd Boy, Kneeling (Large) Hum 260J	*	$345-$370
Shepherd Kneeling, Color Hum 214G	*	$170-$310
Shepherd Kneeling, White Hum 214G	*	$170-$320
Shepherd Kneeling Hum 214G/0	1991	$155
Shepherd Standing Hum 214F/0	1991	$190
Shepherd With Sheep, Color Hum 214F	*	$215-$415
Shepherd With Sheep, White Hum 214F	*	$220-$470
Shepherd, Standing (Large) Hum 260G	*	$590-$650
Stable Hum 260S	*	$480
Virgin Mary, Color Hum 214A	*	$205-$2500
Virgin Mary, White Hum 214A	*	$195-$3000
We Congratulate (Large) Hum 260F	*	$415-$460
We Congratulate, Color Hum 214E	*	$190-$390

Hum No. 435/3/0 *Delicious*, $170-$175

Prices in this Guide

Collectibles on the secondary market sell for a wide range of prices depending upon the venue in which they are sold. M.I. Hummel Figurines in particular, can be found for a small fraction of their value at a garage sale or might break records at an auction. This guide attempts to give the reader the range of values for the M.I. Hummel Figurines which encompasses the oldest known pieces through the currently produced models. Individual figurine models may exist from production in 1935 all the way through to the current year.

Hum No. 460 *Retailer Plaque, Spain*, $300-$1500

Hum No. 471 *Harmony In Four Parts*, $2000-$2500

	Year	Price
M.I. Hummel Nativity		
We Congratulate,		
White Hum 214E	*	**$270-$470**
M.I. Hummel Off To Work		
Fire Fighter Collector's Set	2000	**$205**
In The Kitchen Collector's Set	2000	**$255-$350**
One Coat Or Two?		
Collector's Set	2000	**$255**
Pen Pal Series		
For Mother Hum 257/5/0	1996	**$55**
March Winds Hum 43/5/0	1996	**$55**
One Of You, One Of		
Me Hum 482/5/0	1996	**$55**
Sister Hum 9/5/0	1996	**$55**
Soloist Hum 135/5/0	1996	**$55**
Village Boy Hum 51/5/0	1996	**$55**
Trio Collection		
Traveling Trio Hum 787	1998	**$500**

Due to space constraints, a range of pricing has been provided in some instances. Please consult the 12th edition of Luckey's Hummel® Figurines & Plates Identification and Price Guide for individual pricing based upon trademark variations.

Hum No. 475 *Make A Wish*, $240

Hum No. 483 *I'll Protect Him*, $115

Hum No. 495 *Evening Prayer*, $135

	Year	Price
UNICEF Commemorative Series		
Friends Together 662/0	1994	**$300**
Gentle Fellowship Hum 628	1995	**$550**
We Come In Peace Hum 754	1996	**$385**

Plates

Christmas

Angel	1971	**$20**
Angel With Flute	1972	**$18**
Angelic Gifts	1987	**$52**
Angelic Messenger	1983	**$25**
Angelic Musician	1989	**$75**
Angelic Procession	1982	**$45**
Angel's Light	1990	**$75**
Cheerful Cherubs	1988	**$60**
Christmas Child	1975	**$12**
Gift From Heaven	1984	**$45**
Guardian Angel, The	1974	**$13**
Heavenly Light	1985	**$45**
Heavenly Trio	1978	**$15**
Herald Angel	1977	**$15**
Message From Above	1991	**$75**
Nativity, The	1973	**$60**
Parade Into Toyland	1980	**$25**
Sacred Journey	1976	**$15**

Hum No. 524 *Valentine Gift Doll*, $200-$250

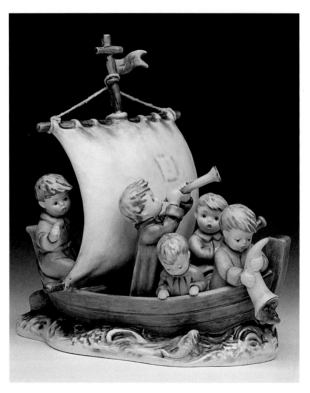

Hum No. 530 *Land In Sight*, $1800-$2250

Hum No. 533 *Ooh, My Tooth*, $145

	Year	Price

Christmas

	Year	Price
Starlight Angel	1979	**$15**
Sweet Blessings	1992	**$75**
Tell The Heavens	1986	**$50**
Time To Remember	1981	**$20**

Figural Christmas Plates

	Year	Price
Christmas Song Hum 692	1996	**$50-$75**
Festival Harmony With Flute Hum 693	1995	**$50-$75**
Thanksgiving Prayer Hum 694	1997	**$50-$75**
Echoes Of Joy Hum 695	1998	**$75-$100**

Four Seasons

	Year	Price
Autumn Glory Hum 299	1999	**$200**
Summertime Stroll Hum 298	1998	**$200**
Winter Melody Hum 296	1996	**$200**

Friends Forever

	Year	Price
For Father Hum 293	1993	**$100-$150**
Meditation Hum 292	1992	**$100-$150**

Due to space constraints, a range of pricing has been provided in some instances. Please consult the 12th edition of Luckey's Hummel® Figurines & Plates Identification and Price Guide *for individual pricing based upon trademark variations.*

Hum No. 534 *A Nap*, $155

Hum No. 545 *Come Back Soon*, $180-$500

Hum No. 556 *One Plus One*, $165-$200

	Year	Price

Friends Forever

Surprise Plate Hum 295	1995	$100-$150
Sweet Greetings		
Plate Hum 294	1994	$100-$150

Kitchen Mould Collection

Baking Day Hum 669	1991	$170-$190
A Fair Measure Hum 670	1991	$170-$190
Sweet As Can Be Hum 671	1991	
For Father Hum 672	1991	$170-$190

Little Companions

Apple Tree Boy And Girl	1991	$45
Budding Scholars	1991	$45
Come Back Soon	1991	$45
Country Crossroad	1991	$45
Hello Down There	1991	$45
Little Explorers	1991	$45
Little Musicians	1991	$45
Private Parade	1991	$45
Squeaky Clean	1991	$45
Stormy Weather	1991	$45
Surprise	1991	$45
Tender Loving Care	1991	$45

Little Homemakers

Chicken Licken Hum 748	1991	$30
Little Sweeper Hum 745	1988	$30

Hum No. 557 *Strum Along,* $155

Hum No. 560 *Lucky Fellow*, $110

Hum No. 561 *Grandma's Girl*, $185

	Year	Price

Little Homemakers

Stitch In Time Hum 747	1990	**$30**
Wash Day Hum 746	1989	**$30**
Band Leader Hum 742	1987	**$30**
Little Fiddler Hum 744	1984	**$30**
Serenade Hum 741	1985	**$30**
Soloist Hum 743	1986	**$30**

M.I. Hummel

Joyful Noise Hum 696	1999	**$75-$100**
Light The Way	2000	**$145**

M.I. Hummel Anniversary Plates

Auf Wiedersehen Hum 282	1985	**$150-$200**
Ring Around The Rosie Hum 281	1980	**$100-$150**
Stormy Weather Hum 280	1975	**$100-$150**

M.I. Hummel Annual Collectible Plates

Apple Tree Boy Hum 270	1977	**$50-$75**
Apple Tree Girl Hum 269	1976	**$50-$75**

Due to space constraints, a range of pricing has been provided in some instances. Please consult the 12th edition of Luckey's Hummel® Figurines & Plates Identification and Price Guide *for individual pricing based upon trademark variations.*

Hum No. 562 *Grandpa's Boy*, $185

Hum No. 574 *Rock-A-Bye*, $1400-$1600

Hum No. 597 *Echoes of Joy*, $130-$140

	Year	Price
M.I. Hummel Annual Collectible Plates		
Bumblebee Friend Hum 923	2002	**$198**
Chick Girl Hum 278	1985	**$50-$75**
Come Back Soon Hum 291	1995	**$175-$250**
Doctor Hum 290	1994	**$150-$200**
Doll Bath Hum 289	1993	**$150-$200**
Farm Boy Hum 285	1989	**$125-$150**
Feeding Time Hum 283	1987	**$250-$300**
Globe Trotter Hum 266	1973	**$150-$200**
Goose Girl Hum 267	1974	**$50-$75**
Happy Pastime Hum 271	1978	**$50-$75**
Hear Ye, Hear Ye Hum 265	1972	**$50-$75**
Heavenly Angel Hum 264	1971	**$500-$750**
Just Resting Hum 287	1991	**$150-$200**
Little Goat Herder Hum 284	1988	**$125-$150**
Little Helper Hum 277	1984	**$50-$75**
Playmates Hum 279	1986	**$200-$250**
Postman Hum 276	1983	**$200-$250**
Ride Into Christmas Hum 268	1975	**$50-$75**
School Girl Hum 273	1980	**$50-$75**
Shepherd's Boy Hum 286	1990	**$150-$200**
Singing Lesson Hum 272	1979	**$40-$60**
Umbrella Boy Hum 274	1981	**$40-$60**
Umbrella Girl Hum 275	1982	**$125-$150**
Wayside Harmony Hum 288	1992	**$150-$200**

Hum No. 621 *At Grandpa's*, $1500-$1600

Hum No. 449 *The Little Pair*, $225-$400

Hum No. 628 *Gentle Fellowship*, $550

	Year	Price

M.I. Hummel Christmas Plates

Angel Duet	1988	$50
Celestial Musician	1987	$69
Guiding Light	1989	$75
Tender Watch	1990	$75

M.I. Hummel Club Exclusive-Celebration

Daisies Don't Tell Hum 736	1988	$45
It's Cold Hum 735	1989	$45
Valentine Gift Hum 738	1986	$45
Valentine Joy Hum 737	1987	$45

M.I. Hummel Plaques

Artist Plaque Hum 756	1993	$400-$500
M.I. Hummel Dealer's Plaq French Hum 208	1949	$3000-$6000
M.I. Hummel Plaques (In English) Hum 187	1947	$175-$1500
Merry Wanderer Wall Plaque Hum 263	1968	$10,000-$15,000

Due to space constraints, a range of pricing has been provided in some instances. Please consult the 12th edition of Luckey's Hummel® Figurines & Plates Identification and Price Guide *for individual pricing based upon trademark variations.*

Hum No. 633 *I'm Carefree*, $440-$1000

Hum No. 646 *Celestial Musician*, $135

Hum No. 647 *Festival Harmony w/Mandolin*, $135

	Year	Price

M.I. Hummel Club Exclusive-Celebration

Puppy Love, Display Plaque
    Hum 767 — 1995 — **$300-$350**

Star Glazer, Wall Plaque
    Hum 237 — 1954 — **$10,000-15,000**

M.I. Hummel Plaques-British Version

Goebel Authorized Retailer
    Plaq. Hum 460 — 1986 — **$300-$750**

M.I. Hummel Plaques-Dutch Version

Goebel Authorized Retailer
    Plaq. Hum 460 — 1986 — **$300-$1500**

M.I. Hummel Plaques-French Version

Goebel Authorized Retailer
    Plaq. Hum 460 — 1986 — **$750-$1000**

M.I. Hummel Plaques-German Version

Goebel Authorized Retailer
    Plaq. Hum 460 — 1986 — **$750-$1000**

M.I. Hummel Plaques-Italian Version

Goebel Authorized Retailer
    Plaq. Hum 460 — 1986 — **$900-$1500**

M.I. Hummel Plaques Made In Germany

M.I. Hummel Dealer's Plaq
    German Hum 205 — 1949 — **$1400-$1700**

Hum No. 648 *Festival Harmony w/Flute*, $135

Hum No. 669 *Baking Day*, $170-$190

Hum No. 670 *A Fair Measure*, $170-$190

	Year	Price

M.I. Hummel Plaques Made In Sweden

M.I. Hummel Dealer's
Plaq Swed. Hum 209 — 1949 — **$4000-$6000**

M.I. Hummel Plaques Schmid Bros.

M.I. Hummel Dealer's
Plaq/Schmid Hum 210 — 1935 — **$20,000-$25,000**

M.I. Hummel Plaques-Spanish Version

Goebel Authorized Retailer
Plaq. Hum 460 — 1986 — **$300-$1500**
M.I. Hummel Dealer's Plaq
Span. Hum 213 — 1951 — **$8000-$10,000**

M.I. Hummel Plaques-Swedish Version

Goebel Authorized Retailer
Plaq. Hum 460 — 1986 — **$300-$1000**

Ornaments

M. I. Hummel

Celestial Musician
Hum 578 — 2002 — **$55**

Due to space constraints, a range of pricing has been provided in some instances. Please consult the 12th edition of Luckey's Hummel® Figurines & Plates Identification and Price Guide for individual pricing based upon trademark variations.

Hum No. 671 *Sweet As Can Be*, $170-$190

Hum No. 672 *For Father*, $170-$190

Hum No. 735
It's Cold, $45

Hum No. 736
*Daisies Don't
Tell*, $45

	Year	Price

M. I. Hummel

	Year	Price
Christmas Song Ornament Hum 879/A	2002	**$20**
Christmas Surprise Hum 536/3/0/0	2002	**$80**
Christmas Time Hum 2106/0	2002	**$93**
Christmas Wish Hum 2094/0	2002	**$80**
Festival Harmony With Flute Hum 577	2002	**$55**
Festival Harmony With Mandolin Hum 576	2002	**$55**
Hear Ye, Hear Ye Lantern Hum 880/A	2002	**$20**
Heavenly Angel Hum 575	2002	**$55**
Ring In The Season Pinecone Hum 2129/A	2002	**$20**

M. I. Hummel Ball Ornaments

	Year	Price
Angel Duet Hum 3016	2002	**$49**
Angel Serenade Hum 3017	2002	**$49**
Celestial Musician Hum 3012	2002	**$49**
Christmas Angel Hum 3015	2002	**$49**
Christmas Song Hum 3018	2002	**$49**
Festival Harmony With Flute Hum 3019	2002	**$49**
Festival Harmony With Mandolin Hum 3020	2002	**$49**

Hum No. 741 *Serenade*, $30

Hum No. 742 *Band Leader*, $30

1871 · W. Goebel Porzellanfabrik · 1996

Hum No. 751 *Love's Bounty*, **$1600-$1800**

	Year	Price
M. I. Hummel Ball Ornaments		
Heavenly Angel Hum 3021	2002	**$49**
M.I. Hummel		
Joyful Noise Hum 598	1999	**$125**
Light The Way	2000	**$125**
M.I. Hummel Annual Figurine Ornaments		
Angelic Guide Hum 571	1991	**$125-$200**
Flying High Hum 452	1988	**$175-$300**
Herald On High Hum 623	1993	**$175-$200**
Light Up The Night Hum 622	1992	**$125-$150**
Love From Above Hum 481	1989	**$125-$150**
Peace On Earth Hum 484	1990	**$125-$150**
M.I. Hummel Century Collection		
Echoes Of Joy Hum 597	1998	**$130-$140**
M.I. Hummel Christmas Bell Ornaments		
Celestial Musician Hum 779	1993	**$30**
Christmas Song Hum 782	1996	**$30**

> *Due to space constraints, a range of pricing has been provided in some instances. Please consult the 12th edition of* Luckey's Hummel® Figurines & Plates Identification and Price Guide *for individual pricing based upon trademark variations.*

Values

The values listed in this guide are a just that "a guide." Prices at retail and on the secondary market may vary from those published here depending on the region and demand for a particular piece.

Hum No. 756 *Artist Plaque*, $400-$500

Hum No. 758 *Nimble Fingers*, $255

Hum No. 759 *To Keep You Warm*, $258-$265

	Year	Price

M.I. Hummel Christmas Bell Ornaments

Festival Harmony With Flute Hum 781	1995	**$30**
Harmony In Four Parts Hum 778	1992	**$28**
Hear Ye, Hear Ye Hum 777	1991	**$28**
Letter To Santa Claus Hum 776	1990	**$28**
Ride Into Christmas Hum 775	1989	**$28**

M.I. Hummel Miniature Ornaments

Celestial Musician Hum 646	1993	**$135**
Festival Harmony With Flute Hum 648	1995	**$135**
Festival Harmony With Mandolin Hum 647	1994	**$135**

Bells

M.I. Hummel

Light The Way	2000	**$70**

M.I. Hummel Annual Bells

Anniversary Bell Hum 730	1985	**$1500-$2000**
Busy Student Hum 710	1988	**$58**
Farewell Hum 701	1979	**$25**
Favorite Pet Hum 713	1991	**$58**
Festival Harmony With Flute Hum 781	1995	**$35**

"Double Crown" Trademark

The very first trademark that was used on the M.I. Hummel Figurines was the "crown" trademark. The Crown was used as the Goebel Company trademark on figurines in the 1930s and 1940s to signify the Goebel family's loyalty to the imperial family of Germany.

In the latter years of the crown tradmark's use, surface stamping became the way to apply the trademark. In some cases, a change from an incised trademark to a surface-stamped version would result in both appearing on the same figurine. Thus the reference to the "double crown" marking, both incised and stamped.

Hum No. 767 *Puppy Love, Display Plaque,* $300-$350

Hum No. 775 *Christmas Bell 1989*, $28

Hum No. 776 *Christmas Bell 1990*, $28

	Year	Price

M.I. Hummel Annual Bells

	Year	Price
In Tune Hum 703	1981	**$38**
Knit One Hum 705	1983	**$35**
Latest News Hum 711	1989	**$58**
Let's Sing Hum 700	1978	**$38**
Mountaineer Hum 706	1984	**$35**
She Loves Me Hum 704	1982	**$35**
Sing Along Hum 708	1986	**$58**
Sweet Song Hum 707	1985	**$35**
Thoughtful Hum 702	1980	**$25**
What's New? Hum 712	1990	**$58**
Whistler's Duet Hum 714	1992	**$58**
With Loving Greetings Hum 709	1987	**$58**

M.I. Hummel Christmas Bells

	Year	Price
Angel With Flute	1972	**$45**
Angelic Gifts	1987	**$48**
Angelic Messenger	1983	**$58**
Angelic Musician	1989	**$53**
Angelic Procession	1982	**$45**

Due to space constraints, a range of pricing has been provided in some instances. Please consult the 12th edition of Luckey's Hummel® Figurines & Plates Identification and Price Guide *for individual pricing based upon trademark variations.*

Hum No. 777 *Christmas Bell 1991*, $28

Hum No. 778 *Christmas Bell 1992*, $28

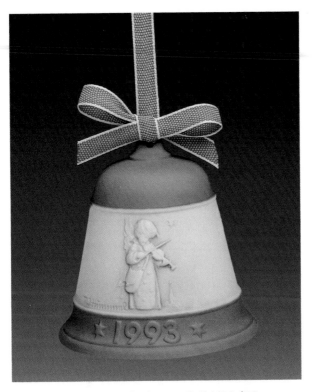

Hum No. 779 *Christmas Bell 1993*, $28

	Year	Price
M.I. Hummel Annual Bells		
Angel's Light	1990	$53
Cheerful Cherubs	1988	$53
Christmas Bell Hum 775	1989	$28
Christmas Bell Hum 776	1990	$28
Christmas Bell Hum 777	1991	$28
Christmas Bell Hum 778	1992	$28
Christmas Bell Hum 779	1993	$28
Christmas Bell Hum 780	1994	$28
Christmas Bell Hum 781	1995	$28
Christmas Bell Hum 782	1996	$28
Christmas Child, The	1975	$47
Echoes Of Joy Hum 784	1998	$28
Gift From Heaven	1984	$45
Guardian Angel, The	1974	$47
Heavenly Light	1985	$80
Heavenly Trio	1978	$45
Herald Angel	1977	$45
Joyful Noise Hum 785	1999	$28
Message From Above	1991	$58
Nativity	1973	$45
Parade Into Toyland	1980	$45
Sacred Journey	1976	$45
Starlight Angel	1979	$47
Sweet Blessings	1992	$65
Tell The Heavens	1986	$47
Time To Remember	1981	$45

Hum No. 780 *Christmas Bell 1994*, $28

Hum No. 781 *Christmas Bell 1995*, $28

Hum No. 782 *Christmas Bell 1996*, $28

	Year	Price
M.I. Hummel Mother's Day Bells		
Afternoon Stroll	1978	**$47**
Cherub's Gift	1979	**$47**
Devotion For Mothers	1976	**$57**
Flower Basket, The	1982	**$47**
Joy To Share	1984	**$47**
Moonlight Return	1977	**$47**
Mother's Little Helper	1980	**$47**
Playtime	1981	**$47**
Spring Bouquet	1983	**$47**

Dolls & Plush

M.I. Hummel Dolls
Anderl 1718	✻	**$150**
Baby 1101 A-H	✻	**$150**
Baby 1102 A-H	✻	**$150**
Bertl 1503	✻	**$175**
Bertl 1603	✻	**$175**
Bertl 1703	✻	**$175**
Birthday Serenade/Boy	1984	**$275**

Due to space constraints, a range of pricing has been provided in some instances. Please consult the 12th edition of Luckey's Hummel® Figurines & Plates Identification and Price Guide for individual pricing based upon trademark variations.

Hum No. 787 *Traveling Trio*, $500

	Year	Price
M.I. Hummel Dolls		
Birthday Serenade/Girl	1984	**$275**
Brieftrager 1720	*	**$175**
Carnival	1985	**$275**
Chimney Sweep 1908	1964	**$115**
Christl 1715	*	**$150**
Easter Greetings	1985	**$275**
Felix 1608	*	**$175**
Felix 1708	*	**$175**
For Father 1917	1964	**$125**
Franzl 1812	*	**$150**
Ganseliesl 1717	*	**$175**
Goose Girl 1914	1964	**$125**
Gretel 1501	*	**$200**
Gretel 1601	*	**$175**
Gretel 1701	*	**$175**
Gretel 1901	1964	**$160**
Hansel 1504	*	**$200**
Hansel 1604	*	**$175**
Hansel 1704	*	**$175**
Hansel 1902	1964	**$160**
Jackal 1714	*	**$150**
Jackal 1806	*	**$125**
Konditor 1723	*	**$175**
Little Knitter 1905	1964	**$125**
Lost Sheep	1985	**$275**
Lost Stocking 1926	1964	**$125**

The Village Bakery, $50

	Year	Price
M.I. Hummel Dolls		
Mariandl 1713	*	$150
Mariandl 1805	*	$125
Max 1506	*	$200
Max 1606	*	$175
Max 1706	*	$175
Merry Wanderer 1906	1964	$125
Merry Wanderer 1925	1964	$125
Mirzl 1811	*	$150
Nachwachter 1719	*	$175
On Holiday	1984	$275
On Secret Path 1928	1964	$85
Peterle 1710	*	$150
Peterle 1810	*	$150
Postman	1984	$275
Puppenmetterchen 1725	*	$175
Radi-Bub 1724	*	$175
Rosa-Blue Baby 1904/B	1964	$95
Rosa-Pink Baby 1904/P	1964	$95
Rosl 1709	*	$150
Rosl 1801	*	$125
Rosl 1809	*	$150
Rudi 1802	*	$125
School Boy 1910	1964	$130
School Girl 1909	1964	$130
Schorschl 1716	*	$150

	Year	Price
M.I. Hummel Dolls		
Schusterbub	*	**$175**
Seppl 1502	*	**$200**
Seppl 1602	*	**$175**
Seppl 1702	*	**$175**
Seppl 1804	*	**$125**
Signs Of Spring	1985	**$275**
Skihaserl 1722	*	**$175**
Strickliesl 1505	*	**$200**
Strickliesl 1605	*	**$175**
Strickliesl 1705	*	**$175**
Valentine Gift Doll Hum 524	*	**$200-$250**
Visiting An Invalid 1927	1964	**$130**
Vroni 1803	*	**$125**
Wanderbub 1507	*	**$200**
Wanderbub 1607	*	**$175**
Wanderbub 1707	*	**$175**

Due to space constraints, a range of pricing has been provided in some instances. Please consult the 12th edition of Luckey's Hummel® Figurines & Plates Identification and Price Guide *for individual pricing based upon trademark variations.*

Cottages

	Year	Price
Bavarian Village Collection		
Angel's Duet	1996	**$50**
Bench & Pine Tree, The/Set	1996	**$25**
Christmas Mail	1996	**$50**
Company's Coming	1996	**$50**
Sled & Pine Tree, The/Set	1996	**$25**
Village Bakery, The	1996	**$50**
Village Bridge, The	1996	**$25**
Winter's Comfort	1996	**$50**
Bavarian Village Collection		
Wishing Well, The	1996	**$25**
Hummel Accessories		
Large Tree/Sled 91312	1995	**$25**
Small Tree/Bench 91313	1995	**$25**
Village Bridge 91310	1995	**$25**
Wishing Well 91311	1995	**$25**
Hummel's Bavarian Christmas		
All Aboard 79287	*	**$50**
Angel's Duet 79281	1994	**$50**
Bakery, The 79282	1994	**$50**
Company's Coming 79283	1995	**$50**
Little Bootmaker 79288	*	**$50**
Off For The Holidays 79286	*	**$50**
Post Office 79285	1995	**$50**
Winter's Comfort 79284	1995	**$50**

Index

HUM NO.	PAGE NO.	HUM NO.	PAGE NO.	HUM NO.	PAGE NO.
26.	310	44.	274	51 5/0	438
26/I	310	44 A	274	51/2/0.	390
26/0	310	44 B	354	51/3/0.	85, 256, 390
27.	246	45/I color	414	51/I	390
27/3	322	45/I white	414	51/0	390
27/I	322	45/III color	414	52.	257, 290
27/III	322	45/III white	414	52/I	290
28.	392	45/0	414	52/0	290
29.	314	45/0 color	414	53.	318
29/0 314	314	46/I color	418	54.	370
29/I	314	46/I white	418	55.	362
30/0 A&B	250	46/III color	418	56.	274
30/0 A&B red.	250	46/III white	418	56/A	259, 274
30/I A&B red	250	46/0 color	418	56/B	260, 354
31.	370	46/0 white	418	57.	266
32.	247, 334	47.	91, 92, 294	57/2/0.	261, 266
32/I	334	47/3/0.	294	57/I	266
32/0	334	47/II	294	57/0	266
34.	374	47/0	252, 294	58.	91, 92, 354
35.	310	48.	414	58/2/0.	263, 354
35/I	310	48/II	414	58/I	354
35/0	310	48/0	414	58/0	354
36.	310	48/V	414	59.	374
36/I	310	49.	388	60 A&B	278
36/0	249, 310	49/3/0.	253, 388	61 A&B	91, 92, 358
37.	306	49/I	388	62.	298
41.	374	49/0	388	63.	264, 374
42.	251	50.	390	64.	370
42/I	294	50/2/0.	390	65.	265, 278
42/0	294	50/I	390	65/I	278
43.	340	50/0	255, 390	65/0	278
43 5/0	438	51.	84, 86, 390	66.	278